Creating Curricula: Aims, Knowledge and Control

Knowledge has been a defining focus for the curriculum studies field. In the early part of the 21st century convincing arguments were mounted that knowledge needed to be 'brought back in', both to the curriculum of schools and to the attention of curriculum researchers. This book is a result of these arguments, and what some regarded as a 'crisis' in curriculum study related to the growing emphasis on international comparisons between education systems.

The book's most important contribution is to build on seminal work in the sociology and philosophy of education in order to develop new foundations for curriculum study, using the importance of 'transactions' as the context for understanding knowledge in the curriculum.

This book was originally published as a special issue of *The Curriculum Journal*.

Dominic Wyse is Professor of Early Childhood and Primary Education, and Head of the Department of Learning and Leadership at the Institute of Education, University College London, UK. The main focus of his research is curriculum and pedagogy, and key areas of his work include the teaching of writing, reading, and creativity. He is the lead editor of the *SAGE Handbook of Curriculum, Pedagogy and Assessment* (2015), and the co-author of *Teaching English, Language and Literacy – 3rd Edition* (2013). His most recent book is *A Guide to Early Years and Primary Teaching* (2015). He is a fellow of the Academy of Social Sciences and a fellow of the RSA.

Creating Curricula: Aims, Knowledge and Control

Edited by
Dominic Wyse

LONDON AND NEW YORK

First published 2017
by Routledge
2 Park Square, Milton Park, Abingdon, Oxfordshire OX14 4RN
711 Third Avenue, New York, NY 10017

Routledge is an imprint of the Taylor & Francis Group, an informa business

First issued in paperback 2018

Copyright © 2017 BERA

All rights reserved. No part of this book may be reprinted or reproduced or utilised in any form or by any electronic, mechanical, or other means, now known or hereafter invented, including photocopying and recording, or in any information storage or retrieval system, without permission in writing from the publishers.

Notice:
Product or corporate names may be trademarks or registered trademarks, and are used only for identification and explanation without intent to infringe.

British Library Cataloguing in Publication Data
A catalogue record for this book is available from the British Library

ISBN 13: 978-1-138-69362-3 (hbk)
ISBN 13: 978-0-367-02882-4 (pbk)

Typeset in Sabon
by RefineCatch Limited, Bungay, Suffolk

Publisher's Note
The publisher accepts responsibility for any inconsistencies that may have arisen during the conversion of this book from journal articles to book chapters, namely the possible inclusion of journal terminology.

Disclaimer
Every effort has been made to contact copyright holders for their permission to reprint material in this book. The publishers would be grateful to hear from any copyright holder who is not here acknowledged and will undertake to rectify any errors or omissions in future editions of this book.

Contents

Citation Information vii
Notes on Contributors ix

Introduction – Creating curricula: aims, knowledge and control 1
Dominic Wyse, Louise Hayward, Kay Livingston and Steve Higgins

1. What is a curriculum and what can it do? 6
   Michael Young

2. Knowledge and the curriculum 13
   David Scott

3. Pragmatising the curriculum: bringing knowledge back into the curriculum conversation, but via pragmatism 28
   Gert Biesta

4. Downgraded curriculum? An analysis of knowledge in new curricula in Scotland and New Zealand 49
   Mark Priestley and Claire Sinnema

5. An aims-based curriculum illustrated by the teaching of science in schools 75
   Michael J. Reiss and John White

6. Two contrasting Australian Curriculum responses to globalisation: what students should learn or become 89
   Bob Lingard and Glenda McGregor

7. Dysfunctional dichotomies? Deflating bipolar constructions of curriculum and pedagogy through case studies from music and history 110
   Tim Cain and Arthur Chapman

8. Curriculum and assessment reform gone wrong: the perfect storm of GCSE English 129
   Tina Isaacs

Index 147

Citation Information

The chapters in this book were originally published in *The Curriculum Journal*, volume 25, issue 1 (March 2014). When citing this material, please use the original page numbering for each article, as follows:

Editorial
Creating curricula: aims, knowledge, and control
Dominic Wyse, Louise Hayward, Kay Livingston and Steve Higgins
The Curriculum Journal, volume 25, issue 1 (March 2014), pp. 2–6

Chapter 1
What is a curriculum and what can it do?
Michael Young
The Curriculum Journal, volume 25, issue 1 (March 2014), pp. 7–13

Chapter 2
Knowledge and the curriculum
David Scott
The Curriculum Journal, volume 25, issue 1 (March 2014), pp. 14–28

Chapter 3
Pragmatising the curriculum: bringing knowledge back into the curriculum conversation, but via pragmatism
Gert Biesta
The Curriculum Journal, volume 25, issue 1 (March 2014), pp. 29–49

Chapter 4
Downgraded curriculum? An analysis of knowledge in new curricula in Scotland and New Zealand
Mark Priestley and Claire Sinnema
The Curriculum Journal, volume 25, issue 1 (March 2014), pp. 50–75

Chapter 5
An aims-based curriculum illustrated by the teaching of science in schools
Michael J. Reiss and John White
The Curriculum Journal, volume 25, issue 1 (March 2014), pp. 76–89

Chapter 6
Two contrasting Australian Curriculum responses to globalisation: what students should learn or become
Bob Lingard and Glenda McGregor
The Curriculum Journal, volume 25, issue 1 (March 2014), pp. 90–110

Chapter 7
Dysfunctional dichotomies? Deflating bipolar constructions of curriculum and pedagogy through case studies from music and history
Tim Cain and Arthur Chapman
The Curriculum Journal, volume 25, issue 1 (March 2014), pp. 111–129

Chapter 8
Curriculum and assessment reform gone wrong: the perfect storm of GCSE English
Tina Isaacs
The Curriculum Journal, volume 25, issue 1 (March 2014), pp. 130–147

For any permission-related enquiries please visit:
http://www.tandfonline.com/page/help/permissions

Notes on Contributors

Gert Biesta is Professor of Educational Theory and Policy at the Institute of Education and Society, University of Luxembourg. He has published widely on the theory and philosophy of education and the theory and philosophy of educational research. His most recent book, *The Beautiful Risk of Education*, was published in 2014 by Paradigm Publishers, USA.

Tim Cain is Professor in Education at Edge Hill University, UK, where he directs the research centre for schools, colleges, and teacher education. He is an editorial board member of the *International Journal of Music Education* and *British Journal of Music Education*. His research interests include teacher research and knowledge mobilisation and his work in this area has appeared in Croatian, Dutch, German, Italian, Spanish, and Slovene publications.

Arthur Chapman is Senior Lecturer in History Education in the Department of Curriculum Pedagogy and Assessment at the Institute of Education, University of London, UK. Arthur is an associate editor of *Teaching History* and *The International Journal of Historical Learning, Teaching and Research* and a member of the editorial boards of the *International Review of History Education* and *The Curriculum Journal*. His publishing and research supervision focus is history pedagogy and didactics with a particular focus on conceptual development in history and on the use of interactive technologies to support historical learning. He is a trustee of the British Curriculum Foundation.

Louise Hayward is Professor of Curriculum Assessment and Pedagogy in the School of Education, University of Glasgow, UK. Her research interests lie in assessment and transformational change.

Steve Higgins is Professor in the School of Education, Durham University, UK. His research interests include the areas of effective use of information and communications technology (ICT) and digital technologies for learning in schools.

Tina Isaacs is Senior Lecturer at the Institute of Education, University of London, UK. She is the programme director for the MA in Educational Assessment and a Director at the Institute's Centre for Post-14 Research and Innovation. Tina returned to higher education in November 2009, before which she worked for 16 years at the National Council for Vocational Qualifications (NCVQ), the Qualifications and Curriculum Authority (QCA), and the Office of Qualifications and Examinations Regulation (Ofqual) specialising in 14–19 qualifications development, implementation, accreditation, and monitoring.

NOTES ON CONTRIBUTORS

Bob Lingard works in the School of Education at The University of Queensland, Australia. His most recent book is *Politics, Policies and Pedagogies in Education* (2014, Routledge).

Kay Livingston is Professor of Educational Research Policy and Practice at the University of Glasgow, UK. Her work focuses on the development of learning and teaching strategies.

Glenda McGregor is Senior Lecturer in the School of Education and Professional Studies at Griffith University, Australia. Her most recent book, co-authored with Martin Mills, is *Re-engaging Young People in Education* (2014, Routledge).

Mark Priestley is Professor of Education in the School of Education at the University of Stirling, where he is Director of Postgraduate Research. His main research interests concern the school curriculum, and especially the processes of curricular change. He is currently Chair of the Editorial Board of the Scottish Educational Review and a member of the Council of the British Educational Research Association.

Michael J. Reiss is programme director for Research and Development and Professor of Science Education at the Institute of Education, University of London, Vice President and Honorary Fellow of the British Science Association, Honorary Visiting Professor at the universities of Leeds and York and the Royal Veterinary College, Director of the Salters-Nuffield Advanced Biology Project, and an Academician of the Academy of Social Sciences. The former Director of Education at the Royal Society, he has written extensively about curricula, pedagogy, and assessment in science education and has directed a very large number of research, evaluation, and consultancy projects over the past 20 years funded by Research Councils, Government Departments, charities, and international agencies.

David Scott is Professor of Curriculum, Pedagogy and Assessment at the Institute of Education, University of London, UK. Previously, he served as the Acting Dean of Teaching and Learning, the Director of the International Institute for Education Leadership, and Professor of Educational Leadership and Learning, University of Lincoln, UK. His recent research projects include Teacher Cadre Management in Indian Schools, Teaching and Learning in Higher Education, Assessment for Learning in Hong Kong Schools, Curriculum Structures 14–18 in Nayarit State, Mexico, and National Curriculum Standards and Structures in Mexico. His most recently published books are *Researching Education* (with R. Usher, 2011, Continuum), *Education, Epistemology and Critical Realism* (2010, Routledge), and *Critical Essays on Major Curriculum Theorists* (2008, Routledge).

Claire Sinnema is Senior Lecturer in the School of Learning, Development and Professional Practice at the University of Auckland, Australia. Her research focuses on the improvement of teaching and learning in the context of curriculum implementation, teacher professional learning, teacher evaluation, pedagogy, and school leadership. She was recently a principal investigator for the New Zealand Ministry of Education funded Monitoring and Evaluating Curriculum Implementation project.

John White is Emeritus Professor of Philosophy of Education at the Institute of Education, University of London, UK, where he has worked since 1965, before which time he taught in secondary schools and colleges in Britain and France. His interests are in the mind of the learner and in interrelationships among educational aims and applications to school curricula. Recent books include the following: *Education and the End of Work* (1997); *Do Howard Gardner's Multiple Intelligences Add Up?* (1998); *Will the New National Curriculum Live up to its Aims?* (with Steve Bramall, 2000); *The Child's Mind* (2002); *Rethinking the School Curriculum* (ed., 2004); *The Curriculum and the Child* (2005); *Intelligence, Destiny and Education: The Ideological Origins of Intelligence Testing* (2006); *What Schools are For and Why* (2007); *Exploring Well-being in Schools* (2011); and *The Invention of the Secondary Curriculum* (2011).

Dominic Wyse is Professor of Early Childhood and Primary Education, and Head of the Department of Learning and Leadership at the Institute of Education, University College London, UK. The main focus of his research is curriculum and pedagogy, and key areas of his work include the teaching of writing, reading, and creativity. He is the lead editor of the *SAGE Handbook of Curriculum, Pedagogy and Assessment* (2015), and the co-author of *Teaching English, Language and Literacy – 3rd Edition* (2013). His most recent book is *A Guide to Early Years and Primary Education* (2015). He is a fellow of the Academy of Social Sciences and a fellow of the RSA.

Michael Young is Emeritus Professor of Education with the School of Lifelong Education and International Development at the Institute of Education, University of London, UK. His main research interests are in the sociology of knowledge and its application to the curriculum with particular reference to the post compulsory phase of education and training.

INTRODUCTION

Creating curricula: aims, knowledge, and control

Dominic Wyse, Louise Hayward, Kay Livingston and Steve Higgins

In December 2013 a new *Programme for International Student Assessment* (PISA) report was published, complete with its international league tables of educational performance in Mathematics, Reading and Science. The media response was perhaps predictable. In many cases, simple league tables ordered by overall score per country were the crude interpretations of the statistics. Headlines and front pages focused on the apparent success of Asian countries, and on the apparent decline of Finland that had been of such interest because of its previous scores in international league tables (Organisation for Economic Cooperation and Development [OECD], 2013a). Prompted by the media reporting, presidents and education ministers responded with criticism of previous governments' efforts to reform education, and promises of tough action to improve standards. For example, the Daily Mail online reported US Education secretary Arne Duncan saying that, 'The brutal fact here is there are many countries that are far ahead of us and improving more rapidly than we are ... This should be a massive wake up call to the entire country' (Daily Mail, 2013).

This increased focus on international measurement through pupil testing represents a dominant and growing influence on education. More specifically, in relation to the curriculum journal, international measures such as PISA are influencing the ways that policy makers think about curricula. The perception that a particular position in the league tables is correlated with educational standards is often followed by greater control over elements of schooling particularly of national curricula. This control includes greater specification of content of curricula, and over the knowledge to be taught. Aims for the curriculum cease to be democratically developed visions of nations' future citizens, instead aims may be added as an afterthought, or even become articulated as explicit intentions to compete in the global education 'race'.

The performativity pressures outlined above are not only having an impact on political perceptions and education systems, it can also be argued that this new world order (perhaps akin to the *new imperialism* (Tikly, 2004)) has paralleled something of a crisis in curriculum studies. The growing hegemony of political thinking on curriculum and assessment in the twenty-first century is a phenomenon in need of continued critical attention, and insights into more appropriate future directions.

It was in the context of these intersections between international performativity and curriculum studies that the idea for this special issue arose following some early meetings of a new curriculum, pedagogy and assessment special interest group (SIG) of the *British Educational Research Association*. The inaugural seminar of the SIG, held at the *Institute of Education, University of London*, examined what kinds of aims might be appropriate to frame curricula. This was followed by a second seminar, held in Glasgow, that examined synergies for better learning, including reflections by academics, policy makers and practitioners on the OECD report of the same name (OECD, 2013b). Speakers from both these seminars (and other curriculum specialists) were invited to propose papers for the special issue.

The special issue has been designed to contribute to the renaissance in curriculum studies (Priestly & Biesta, 2013). In particular, it examines foundational conceptions that might now inform curriculum study and curricula. At the start of this editorial, we have already alluded to control, in particular the control politicians exert in the context of international comparison. Another foundational curriculum conception is knowledge and its place in curricula. Michael Young has been at the forefront of *Bringing Knowledge Back In* (Young, 2008). In England, his theoretical work has also seen practical application, for example informing the national curriculum of the Conservative-Liberal Democrat government to be implemented by schools in 2014. For this reason, we were delighted by his agreement to provide a commentary on the papers in the special issue.

John Dewey was clear that the best knowledge available to society was the appropriate material for children's learning, but only through teaching that made a connection with children's experiences and thoughts. Dewey argued that good teaching is built on the educator's understanding that there should be an *interaction* between the child's experiences and ideas, and the school's aim to inculcate learning. Less effective learning would take place if, instead of interaction, opposition is built between experience and learning. Dewey also identified what he called the three 'evils' of inappropriate curriculum material: (a) the material is not organic to the child; (b) the connecting links of need and aim are conspicuous by their absence and (c) there is a lack of logical value (Dewey, 1902, p. 24). Logical value to Dewey was curriculum organisation that represented the best knowledge in society organised through authentic hands-on experiences for the child. The teacher's role, however, was vital: 'Guidance [i.e. by the teacher] is not external imposition. *It is freeing the life-process for its own most adequate fulfilment*' [*op. cit.* p. 17 Italics in original].

However, rather than seeing a greater place for Dewian philosophy informing national curriculum thinking in England from 2010 onwards, it was Matthew Arnold who was selected by Education Secretary Michael Gove, in particular Arnold's essay advocating the importance of culture as a remedy for the problems with society, in which he said that we should focus on 'the best which has been thought and said in the world, and, through this knowledge, turning a stream of fresh and free thought upon our stock notions and habits, which we now follow staunchly but mechanically, vainly imagining that there is a virtue in following them staunchly which makes up for the mischief of following them mechanically' (Arnold, 1869, p. 5). The appeal to this kind of theory by the Secretary of State for Education in England was notable, but his early attention to 'the best that has been thought and written' [sic], consistent with the extreme reduction of attention to language in the national curriculum in favour of literacy, rather than an appeal to 'turning a stream of fresh and free thought upon our stock notions and habits' proved to be prescient in relation to the final version of England's national curriculum.

One way of structuring knowledge in the school curriculum is through traditional school subjects. However, Basil Bernstein's attention to *classification* and *framing*, in the context of the structures of power and the principles of social control, included identifying 'some reasons for a movement towards the institutionalising of integrated codes *of the weak classification and framing (teacher and taught)*' (Bernstein, 1971, p. 66). These reasons included recognition that higher levels of thinking were increasingly differentiated; more flexibility was required in the labour force; the need for more egalitarian education; and the need to make sense of major societal problems related to power and control. Bernstein's thinking also focused on ways to 'declassify and so alter power structures and principles of control; in so doing to unfreeze the structuring of knowledge and to change the boundaries of consciousness' (Bernstein, 1971, p. 67). He theorised that only a select few pupils/students are normally allowed access to 'relaxed frames', in other words a state of empowerment for these pupils to 'create endless new realities' as part of the understanding that knowledge is permeable and provisional. Bernstein's chapter was published in the book entitled *Knowledge and Control: New Direction for the Sociology of Education* edited by Michael Young.

Although there is perhaps consensus on the idea that the key role of teaching and learning is communication of knowledge from teacher to learner (but less consensus about knowledge from learner to teacher), there is a need to make progress on what are the most appropriate ways to understand knowledge, and to represent knowledge, in national curricula. The aim of the proposed special issue is to explore theoretical and empirical arguments for the construction of national curricula in order to articulate some parameters around which effective curricula might be built.

We will not introduce the papers individually in this editorial, as Michael Young's commentary serves to do this, instead we briefly address two themes that it seems to us traverse most of the papers. The first issue concerns the overarching thinking that should guide curriculum study and curriculum practice. Indeed the ways that overarching thinking is informed by epistemological choices is addressed directly in one of the papers where it is suggested that such choices should take account of the transitivity of knowledge within disciplines. One possible choice of overarching frame, as we have indicated already, is through a knowledge-based curriculum. But knowledge perhaps should be seen as both constructed *and* real, or as a 'transaction'. In relation to schooling, we are also cautioned to remember that although disciplines are the basis for knowledge this does not mean that school subjects are necessarily the most appropriate way to organise knowledge in the school curriculum. Indeed it is also argued that curriculum development should begin with aims not with subjects. The second theme that spans most of the papers in the special issue is one that we began the editorial with, international performativity and the curriculum. The nature of globalisation and its extent is a topic of intense speculation but evidence continues to accumulate of its impact on education and of the need for new ways of conceptualising policy analysis (Ball, 2012). The complexity of the global influences on curriculum are seen through analyses in the special issue that include historical political contexts, for example showing global influences contributing to confused attempts at shaping the individual person through a curriculum.

Consistent with our aim to relate theories and empirical work to policy and practice the papers to varying degrees suggest new ways of thinking to inform teaching and learning. More specifically an account is given which takes the theoretical problem of dichotomies, such as formal/informal learning, and critically explores these in relation to two school subjects. Finally, in an analysis of the changes to the GCSE exam in England we see the risks and consequences of poorly conceived assessment changes. Historically, the performativity of high stakes assessment has had a dominant influence on curriculum, evident in the nature of international and national assessment systems, and evident in the expertise of the people who have influenced and led curriculum development (early examples include Bloom, 1956, and Tyler, 1949). Our commitment to exploration of theory/research and policy/practice synergies is also seen in a review of Reiss and White's book that argues for an aims-based curriculum. In these reviews, the voices of an academic and a practitioner are heard; it is clear that the 'sharp end' of heavy handed top-down political control of the curriculum is most unwelcome.

The special issue and this editorial are indicative of the editors' vision for the journal. We welcome and encourage perspectives from different disciplines, theoretical and empirical. The special issue includes strong contributions, sometimes conflicting, from philosophical, sociological and multi-disciplinary perspectives. We hope the work exemplifies the idea that curriculum is such an important element it can be seen as the sine qua non of education as a discipline (and we use the word 'discipline' intentionally). We are immensely grateful to all the contributors of this work, and we hope that our readers will take up the challenge of many of the topics it raises.

References

Arnold, M. (2009 [originally published 1869]). *Culture and anarchy*. Oxford: Oxford University Press.

Ball, S. (2012). *Global education Inc.: New policy networks and the neo-liberal imaginary*. London: Routledge.

Bernstein, B. (1971). On the classification and framing of educational knowledge. In M. Young (Ed.), *Knowledge and control: New directions for the sociology of education* (pp. 47 69). London: Collier MacMillan Ltd.

Bloom, B. S. (Ed.). (1956). *Taxonomy of educational objectives. Book 1 cognitive domain*. New York: Longman/David McKay Company, Inc.

Daily Mail Online (2013). 'Wake up call': President Obama vows to improve US education after underwhelming results in global examinations. Retrieved from http://www.dailymail.co.uk/news/article-1336488/Obama-vows-improve-US-education-poor-results-global-examinations.html

Dewey, J. (1902). *The child and the curriculum*. Chicago: The University of Chicago Press.

Organisation for Economic Cooperation and Development (OECD). (2013a). *World reaction to PISA*. Paris: Author. Retrieved from http://www.oecd.org/education/focus-world-reaction-to-pisa.htm

Organisation for Economic Cooperation and Development (OECD). (2013b). *Synergies for better learning: An international perspective on assessment and evaluation*. Paris: Author.

Priestly, M., & Biesta, G. (Eds.). (2013). *Reinventing the curriculum: New trends in curriculum policy and practice*. London: Bloomsbury.

Tikly, L. (2004). Education and the new imperialism. *Comparative Education, 40*(2), 173 198.

Tyler, R. (1949). *Basic principles of curriculum and instruction*. Chicago: University of Chicago Press.

Young, M. (2008). *Bringing knowledge back in: From social constructivism to social realism in the sociology of education*. London: Routledge.

What is a curriculum and what can it do?

Michael Young

Institute of Education, University of London

Despite the widespread use of the term 'curriculum' in educational research and policy, the questions in my title are not easy to answer. Furthermore, as is indicated by the papers in this Special Issue, there is little consensus among specialists in the field. An attempt to answer them, however, is worthwhile because much writing and research about the curriculum is devoted to saying what it ought to do, and what its aims are, with less regard for what exactly a curriculum is that might fulfil those aims.

My starting point is that curricula are 'social facts' in the sense used by the French sociologist and Professor of Pedagogy, Emile Durkheim (Durkheim, 1938). What this means is that a curriculum as a 'social fact' is never reducible to the acts, beliefs or motivation of individuals; it is a structure that constrains not only the activities of those involved – primarily teachers and students, but also those who design curricula or attempt to achieve certain goals with them. However, curricula are not only constraints on our actions. They make some things possible to learn that most of us would find impossible to learn without them; at the same time they set limits on what is possible to learn in schools or other educational institutions. In this way curricula are like other 'specialised' institutions – families and businesses, for example – they have particular purposes. It follows, as Reiss and White note in their paper, that contemporary curricula, and their constituent elements such as subjects, inevitably rely on earlier curricula, either because they are taken for granted as 'the only way to organise the transmission of knowledge or because they have demonstrated their capacity to be effective instruments for learning. In a sense this merely recognises the central role of curricula in the transmission of knowledge from one generation to the next. A curriculum does not imply a particular model of pedagogy; however, they vary in the extent to which they pre-suppose assumptions about whether learners vary in their capabilities. Whether the focus is on the curriculum of an individual school or on the National Curriculum of a country, both are structures designed for particular purposes. The debates, which many of the papers in this Special

Issue refer to and take sides on, are about these purposes. There is one question which runs through all the papers, albeit in very different ways. It is the extent to which *assumptions about knowledge* define the curriculum as a structure, and, as none of the papers deny the importance of knowledge, what exactly these assumptions are. In prefacing my brief comments on the individual papers, I want to suggest that seeing the curriculum as a 'structure' offering constraints and possibilities may be a useful way of considering the aims/knowledge debate introduced by Reiss and White and the more overtly political questions about how and by whom curricular decisions are made.

From their earliest days, and increasingly in modern societies, schools have been established as *specialised institutions*, which can realise some aims and not others. For example, it is possible for a curriculum to be oriented to students acquiring knowledge of mathematics or history or a particular set of religious beliefs; however, it makes no sense to conceive of a curriculum enabling young people to get jobs when the primary influence on whether a young person gets a job is the quantity and quality of jobs available. The logic of recognising the *specialist* role of schools and the curriculum can be illustrated in another way. No one could disagree with Reiss and White that schools should promote well-being and human flourishing in what they do; however, that is what we expect of institutions that do not have curricula such as families, towns and businesses. What distinguishes schools is that their primary concern, as embodied in the specialist professional staff they recruit, and in their curriculum, is (or should be) to provide all their students with access to knowledge. As Ruth Cigman has pointed out human flourishing pre-supposes access to knowledge (Cigman, 2012). It is a school's curriculum that addresses the question 'what knowledge?'; an issue explored in considerable depth in the first paper in this issue by David Scott.

The curriculum as a social fact, I suggest, acts as a constraint on what students can learn, not the least both through its boundaries or lack of them between subjects and between the curriculum and the experience of students out of school. However these boundaries are not just constraints, they are also a set of possibilities not only about what students can learn but about how they can progress in their learning. The extent to which these possibilities are achievable by a school and by what proportion of pupils will depend on a range of factors. Some will be *internal* to the school, such as the approach to curriculum leadership of the headteacher and her/his team of senior teachers and the range of expertise of the whole staff; and some will be *external* such as the wider distribution of opportunities in the society as a whole and in the local catchment area of the school. What uniquely schools can do for all pupils, and that is why the curriculum is the pre-eminent issue for all of us in education, is to offer opportunities for pupils at all ages to move beyond the experience they bring to school and to acquire knowledge that is not tied to that experience. It is this (relatively) context-free knowledge, which some of us have described as 'powerful knowledge' (Beck, 2013; Young, 2013; Young & Muller, 2013), and which, in Basil Bernstein's words enables students to 'think the un-thinkable and the not yet thought' (Wheelahan, 2012). This is the promise that schooling and its main instrument, the curriculum offers. How this promise works out and for whom, and why it is un-realised for so many students is what the papers in this Special Issue are concerned with; I turn, therefore, to consider the papers, briefly, in turn.

The first paper by David Scott presents a systematic review of the different ways curriculum theorists have conceptualised knowledge. From the perspective developed here, his most important conclusion derives from his premise that all human learning is an 'epistemic' or 'knowledge building' activity. It follows that the curriculum can be understood as a structure or instrument for extending that epistemic activity beyond the 'knowledge building' that pupils are involved in their everyday lives. Any other rationale for the curriculum would be a denial, at least for some, of the entitlement of all pupils to extend their unique human capacity for 'epistemic activity' and 'knowledge building'. This entitlement is limited, in principle, by two features of all curricula, the nature of knowledge itself and what we know about how it is acquired.

The second paper by Gert Biesta tackles the issue of 'knowledge building' from a quite different perspective. He makes the case for Dewey's 'transactional realism' as a way of tackling the relation between knowledge and experience which he rightly sees as the key issue for curriculum and pedagogic theory and practice. Early in his paper Biesta states that he wants to avoid the recent tendency for educational theory to 'lose' knowledge and slip into what he has elsewhere described as 'learnification' (Biesta 2010a). To do this he introduces Dewey's concepts of 'coordination' and 'transaction' as a way of bridging the separation of knowledge and experience that all pupils face on entering school and engaging with the curriculum. However, while the concept of 'transaction' identifies a process, it is not clear how it allows for a discussion of *what* is being transacted; this means that we are in danger of being left with a theory of pedagogy, or teaching and learning but with no curriculum. Second, Biesta reminds us that Dewey was concerned with how an 'absolutist' scientific world view (today, we might call it 'positivist') was colonising other alternatives in education; something one can recognise in much current educational research. However, as Biesta explains, Dewey was far from being anti-science and he tried to construct what he saw as a more adequate, 'non-absolutist' conception of science. The problem for curriculum theorists is that Dewey (and Biesta seems not to disagree) does not distinguish between his concept of science and 'intelligent common sense'. For Dewey, we are or should be all, in this sense, 'scientists'.

This collapse of the differences between scientific thinking and common sense leaves one with wondering where this takes us in thinking about the curriculum. Whatever else it is, the curriculum is surely more than an extension of common sense.

In his concluding discussion Biesta suggests that the social realist approach to knowledge and the curriculum that I and others have developed from Durkheim can be located in what he describes as the 'domain of certainty' rather than the 'domain of possibility' and that it thus it leads to an inescapable determinism. However, as Moore (2011) expresses more clearly than most, a realist sociology of knowledge is committed to the 'fallibility' of knowledge not its 'certainty'. In other words, even truth in the mathematical sciences is no more than 'the best knowledge we have so far'. All knowledge, however reliable, is always challengeable because it is no more than our best attempt to make sense of that which is external to us – the real world. Hence it is in the 'domain of possibility' not the 'domain of certainty'.

In the third paper, Priestley and Sinnema begin by questioning some of the assumptions underpinning the case for a knowledge-led curriculum. The strength of their paper is that they go beyond the theoretical debates and test some of these assumptions by analysing documents from two recently reformed National Curricula in Scotland and New Zealand. In asking the question 'do these new curricula downgrade knowledge?' they demonstrate that although the word 'knowledge' is frequently mentioned in the documents, it tends to be under-specified and the acquisition of knowledge is invariably associated with a variety of other educational purposes. In other words, the evidence from the two curricula studied gives some support to the 'downgrading' argument. This is an important beginning. However, to take the questions they raise further will undoubtedly require greater precision in defining the term knowledge than can be achieved by counting the number of times the word is used. This takes us back to the issues about what the word knowledge implies that David Scott's paper raised.

Priestley and Sinnema's paper raises a number of other questions about the idea of a knowledge-led curriculum which warrants further exploration. Both the New Zealand and Scottish curricula appear to put more emphasis *how children should be* rather than on *what they are expected to know*. This is consistent with the view that schools should not only provide opportunities for students to acquire knowledge but that they should develop 'their attributes and dispositions... and teach everyday knowledge that has practical utility for everyday life'. However everyday knowledge is what all pupils bring to school and it is difficult to see why it would need teaching. There is a danger that such a view can slip into treating the role of the curriculum as repairing deficiencies in the pre-school identities of pupils, rather than taking them beyond those identities, as recent research in New Zealand shows (Sitein, 2013).

Priestley and Sinnema suggest that the distinction between everyday and disciplinary knowledge and the related distinction between knowledge and skills are not as clear cut as is suggested by those who argue for a knowledge-led curriculum. This may well be true; however, it does not negate the strengths of the distinctions provided they are treated analytically and not descriptively. They also suggest that it is perfectly possible to conceive of alternative but equally rigorous approaches to introducing disciplinary knowledge that are not framed as traditional subjects. However, even if we accept this possibility, the pedagogic problems posed by *any* form of rigorous knowledge, which cannot avoid being at odds with the experience that pupils bring to school, remain.

Reiss and White restate White's now familiar case (Reiss & White, 2013) for an aims-based curriculum and apply it to the specific case of science teaching. The 'pros' and 'cons' of an aims-based approach to the curriculum have been extensively debated and are beyond the scope if this short paper. However, there are two crucial questions facing science educators that their proposal for an aims-based approach to the curriculum does not seem to address. The first issue is whether a science curriculum for all should be based on an introduction to the concepts and methods of physics, chemistry and biology. The counter view is that such a 'foundational' approach is only appropriate for those planning in the future to specialise in one or more of the sciences. The related question is, if such a 'foundation' is not appropriate for the majority of pupils who are unlikely to be future specialists, does this not imply that the science curriculum must be differentiated at some relatively early stage of secondary schooling? A differentiated curriculum raises the question as to the basis on which pupils are selected (or allowed to choose) their curriculum and the principles on which the curriculum is differentiated? The fate of the Schools Council's Project *Science for the Young School Leaver* in the 1960s and 1970s is not a happy precedent for a differentiated secondary science curriculum.

Lingard and McGregor locate the 'knowledge/curriculum' debate in the broad context of the social changes associated with globalisation and the new demands that these changes are thought to place on the curriculum for the future cohorts of those leaving school. They compare two very different approaches to the curriculum developed in Australia; Queensland's 'new basics' and the proposals by the Australian Curriculum, Assessment and Reporting Authority (ACARA) for a Federal Curriculum for all states. Broadly summarised, 'new basics' was a radical approach to a skills-led curriculum which gave considerable autonomy to individual schools and encouraged them to become more closely involved in their communities – a proposal not unlike the Royal Society for the encouragement of Arts, Manufactures and Commerce (RSA's) less systematically developed Opening Minds curriculum in England. However, as Lingard and McGregor point out, the 'new basics' curriculum was only developed as a pilot for only 36 schools and with the massive swing to the Right in Queensland in the recent state elections, it is highly unlikely to be extended to the state as a whole. The ACARA curriculum signifies a 'return to subjects' but this is combined with basic skills testing in the early years of secondary schooling. The paper does not go into detail about the 'new basics curriculum or the idea of 'productive learning' associated with it; its strengths are that it brings out clearly the complex interweaving of political and curricular ideologies as well as their links to broader political and economic changes.

Cain and Chapman's paper addresses a familiar educational issue, the seductive popularity of such dichotomies as content/skills and formal/informal, and explores it in relation to two subjects, history and music as contrasting case studies. I do not have the expertise to comment on the paper's accounts of the two subjects, so I will restrict my comments to their broader issue of the role of dichotomies in educational research. They begin with Robin Alexander's argument that dichotomies 'reduce complex educational debates to bipolar slogans cast in a state of permanent and irreconcilable opposition' and go on to question his solution – replacing bipolar distinctions by a sixfold typology. In this they are surely right – such a sixfold typology can only complicate existing complexity. Their preferred alternative is a 'middle-ground' approach that frames dichotomous concepts as a tension between different, but not necessarily competing ideas. This is a important step; however, it might be taken further in clarifying the difference between their approach and the way dichotomous concepts tend to be used in educational research, by drawing the German sociologist, Max Weber's concept of an 'ideal type' (Weber, 1949).

Weber recognised that dichotomies in the social sciences and in (by implication) educational research are in many cases all we have. We do not have concepts that are conceptually related in precise ways and have clear empirical referents – like mass and weight or temperature and heat in physics. Weber suggested that descriptive dichotomies could be reformulated in the social sciences as *ideal types* indicating tendencies. For example, let us take the curriculum/pedagogy dichotomy that a number of papers in this Special Issue refer to. Teachers draw on the school curriculum and their knowledge of pedagogy in their teaching; for them the two are not distinct. However, in designing curricula, training teachers or undertaking curriculum research, an *analytical* distinction between the two concepts (as ideal types) may be useful. As an ideal type, the concept 'curriculum' refers to the knowledge that it is hoped pupils will acquire by the end of a course. In contrast, pedagogy refers to the activities that teachers devise for their pupils to enable them to acquire the knowledge specified by the curriculum. This does not make the two concepts separate in the practice of teachers. What such analytical distinctions can do is to identify tendencies and question the way concepts are used as descriptions or even dogmas – an example is that between knowledge-centred and learner-centred curricula. No curricula can disregard the knowledge it is hoped that students will acquire. Acquiring knowledge always involves concepts (in other words, knowing something), but it also involves practical activities – using concepts to explain something or solve a problem (in other words, skills or doing something). The distinction between knowledge and skills is useful analytically, as a pair of ideal types, but not as a description or as a slogan to identify whether something is 'good' or 'bad'.

The final paper by Tina Isaacs is a cautionary tale for curriculum specialists, both theorists and policy-makers, who forget the extent to which, in the English system, curriculum decisions at every level, from government to classroom teacher, are shaped to a considerable degree by the examination system, even though the two are often thought about and analysed quite independently. Isaacs presents a detailed and compelling case study of recent changes in General Certificate of Seconday Education (GCSE) English assessment and grading that she describes as a 'perfect storm'. She uses the example to argue that the problems of grade inflation that the government's latest reforms are designed to overcome, are all too likely to recur, albeit in a slightly different way.

Together these papers offer a welcome change from the ideological positioning that has characterised much of what passes for 'debate' between the present Government and the educational community in the last three years. In stepping back from any easy labelling of positions, they point to an agenda for curriculum research that could remind any Government that curriculum theory and research is a specialist resource they can ill afford to neglect.

References

Beck, J. (2013). Powerful knowledge, esoteric knowledge, curriculum knowledge. *Cambridge Journal of Education*, *43*(2), 177 193.
Biesta, G.J.J. (2010a). *Good education in an age of measurement: Ethics, politics, and democracy*. Boulder, CO: Paradigm Publishers.
Cigman, R. (2012). We need to talk about wellbeing. *Research Papers in Education*, *27*, 4, 449 462.
Durkheim, E. (1938). *The rules of sociological method*. New York, NY: Free Press.
Moore, R. (2011). *Towards a sociology of truth*. London: Continnum.
Reiss, M., & White, J. (2013). *An aims-based curriculum: The significance of human flourishing for schools*. London: IOE Press.
Sitein, A. (2013). Positive in their own identities?: Social studies and identity affirmation. *New Zealand Journal of Educational Studies*, *48*(2).
Weber, M. (1949). *The methodology of the social sciences*. New York, NY: Free Press.
Wheelahan, L. (2012). The problem with competency-based training. In H. Lauder & Young, M., Daniels, H., and Balarin, M. (Eds.), *Education for the knowledge economy? Critical perspectives*. London: Routledge.
Young, M. (2013). Powerful knowledge: An analytically useful concept or just a 'sexy sounding term'? *Cambridge Journal of Education*, *43*(2), 131 136.
Young, M., & Muller, J. (2013). On the powers of powerful knowledge. *Review of Education*, *2*(1), 229 250.

Knowledge and the curriculum

David Scott

Department of Learning, Curriculum and Communication, Institute of Education, University of London, London, UK

> The article focuses on knowledge and how it relates to the school curriculum. This means that a reason (or reasons) for designating knowledge as the central dimension of the curriculum has to be provided. Two reason-giving arguments can be invoked to support this proposition. The first is to conceptualise learning as an epistemic activity, and the second is to suggest that those curriculum ideologies which marginalise knowledge are deficient or inadequate. It is then necessary to determine what this knowledge-producing activity is, and to distinguish it from those curriculum ideologies which purport to prioritise knowledge but rarely achieve their aim. The issues of how knowledge is transformed at the pedagogic and evaluative sites, and the relationship between these three sites, are also briefly addressed.

Introduction

This article offers a set of reasons for placing knowledge at the centre of a curriculum and it makes the following argument. A curriculum, which is a set of teaching and learning prescriptions, is in essence a knowledge-forming activity. However, this cannot resolve the issue of what should be included in that curriculum and what should be excluded from it. The next step then is to determine what might constitute a legitimate form of knowledge and thus by implication an illegitimate form. Three epistemic frameworks: foundationalism, instrumentalism and pragmatism are examined for their capacity to act as curriculum rationales. Finally, a variety of social epistemologies are identified and investigated: social constructivism, social realism, epistemic realism, inferentialism and critical realism, and though parts of these theories are understood as useful for the task in hand, it is suggested that on their own they do not amount to a complete theory of knowledge and therefore of learning. However, elements of each of the epistemic frameworks set out above (i.e. foundationalism, instrumentalism and pragmatism), it is suggested, can contribute to a coherent and comprehensive theory of curriculum and provide a reason or set of reasons as to why a curriculum should include some items and reject others, and what shape and form it should take.

Axiomatically then, a school curriculum is always a selection from a range of cognitions, skills or dispositions that are available within a society; that is, these are being, or have been, manifested in human practices of a discursive, institutional, agential or embodied kind. Choices also have to be made as to how a curriculum is constructed; that is, what relations are considered to be appropriate between the contents of the curriculum, its pedagogic forms, its learning strategies, and its evaluative criteria and apparatus. These choices of cognitions, skills and dispositions then, if they are to be considered reasonable, or at least in Sellars' (1997, p. 89) terms, able to be placed within 'the logical space of reasons', require a justification or rationale for them as curricular contents. This justification can take an epistemic form: a curriculum is in essence a framework for some type of learning or another; learning whether cognitive, skill-based or dispositional is understood as a knowledge-development activity; and therefore knowledge is central to the construction and realisation of the curriculum. However, it then becomes necessary to determine what this knowledge is, and how it is formed and legitimated.

Learning, or so it can be argued, is an epistemic or knowledge-producing activity. An accepted, but not uncontested, view of learning is to theorise it as a process, with a range of characteristics. It has a set of pedagogic relations, in that it incorporates a relationship between a learner and a catalyst, such as a person, a text, an object in nature, a particular array of resources, an artefact, an allocation of a role or function to a person, or a sensory object. A change process is required, either internal to the learner or external to the community of which this learner is a member. In any learning episode, there are temporal and spatial arrangements, and these can be understood in two ways: first, that learning is internally structured, and second, that learning episodes are externally located in time and place. Learning is conditioned by arrangements of embodied, discursive, institutional or agential resources, and this has implications for the types of learning that can take place. Each learning episode has socio-historical roots. What is learnt in the first place is formed in society and outside the individual. It is shaped by the life that the person is leading. Learning then has an internalisation element, where what is formally external to the learner is interiorised by the learner, and a performative element, where what is formally internal to the learner is exteriorised by the learner in the world. These elements of learning if and as they are realised constitute a knowledge-forming activity.

Knowledge is therefore central to the three types of learning identified above: cognitive, skill-based and dispositional. Cognition comprises the manipulation of those symbolic resources (words, numbers, pictures, etc.) which point to (though not necessarily in a mirroring or isomorphic sense) something outside itself, though the referent might also be construed as internally related (for example, cf. Brandom, 2000). Skill-based knowledge is different from cognition because it is procedural and not declarative, though the purely skill-based competency curriculum which underpins an international comparative system of testing such as the Programme for International Student Assessment (PISA) (Organisation for Economic Cooperation and Development [OECD], 2009) would mistakenly reject this distinction and its designation as an epistemic activity. Distinguishing between knowledge of how to do something and knowledge of something is important but both are in essence knowledge-making activities. Dispositional knowledge refers to relatively stable habits of mind and body, sensitivities to occasion and participation repertoires. These three types of knowledge therefore have different forms in their original states and as a result different pedagogic structures, different expressive or performative modes, and can only be assessed functionally in relation to their different internal relations; that is, there have to be different ways of assessing or evaluating them.

Any knowledge-forming activity, whether cognitive, skill-based or dispositional, needs a reason or set of reasons as to why the production of this form of knowledge should be preferred to the production of other possible forms. A counter-argument to this is to suggest that knowledge is intrinsically worthwhile and therefore does not require a justification or even a procedure for selection. And this then provides a way of determining the contents of a curriculum. The argument is that if someone chooses to dispute or deny the claim that the pursuit of knowledge is intrinsically worthwhile, then it follows that they are being inconsistent, because in asking this question, they are already committed to its pursuit and thus have already answered the question. As White (1982) suggests, this argument is flawed in so far as asking the particular question about the pursuit of knowledge in a general sense does not commit one to the pursuit of all types of knowledge per se; and furthermore, does not provide a justification for deciding that some types of knowledge are more worthwhile than other types of knowledge. Thus, even if the first part of the argument is accepted, there are no grounds within the argument presented here for determining what that knowledge should be. And though this in principle is an argument in favour of knowledge it is not an argument which can determine what should be included in, and consequently excluded from, a curriculum.

In order to provide a rationale or justification for these inclusions and exclusions, it is important to determine what that knowledge is and how it can be constituted. This activity involves the acceptance of certain types of knowledge and the subsequent rejection of others. For example, knowledge which is understood as being determinate (there is a singular truth which can be known), rational (there are no contradictory explanations), impersonal (the more objective and the less subjective the better), verificationist (the meaning of statements about human behaviours and their origins are understood in terms of observational or experimental data) and predictive (explanations of human behaviours are knowledge claims formulated as generalisations from which predictions can be made, and events and phenomena controlled) is fundamentally different from knowledge which is retroductively produced and referenced to a social world which is stratified, open and has ontological depth (cf. Bhaskar, 2010), and thus a belief in both of these is difficult to sustain. Another example refers to the nature of knowledge, and, in particular, whether it is individual or social. Standard epistemology construes the conditions for justified belief in individualist terms, rather than placing it within social contexts. This can be contrasted with social epistemologies (cf. Vygotsky, 1987) which prioritise the social over the individual.

Knowledge (whether we are referring here to its essence, its legitimacy or its genealogy) is contested and thus requires choices to be made between these different formulations, conceptions and arrangements. This in turn has implications for the types of pedagogy that can be employed and the types of evaluative procedures that should be adopted. This is predicated on an assumption that learning per se is always about learning something which we might want to call knowledge; binding knowledge and learning closely together then is an acknowledgement that knowledge can be declarative, procedural or embodied and that in its production it can be construed as a learning activity.

Foundationalism

A common argument which purportedly allows one to distinguish between legitimate and illegitimate items in a curriculum is foundationalist in orientation. Foundationalist views of epistemology were developed in response to radical sceptical beliefs about the possibility of having secure knowledge of the world; indeed the argument the sceptic made was that such knowledge is fundamentally impossible. If we choose to subscribe to a relativist epistemology and thus accept that our descriptions of reality are relative to particular and specific time- and space-bound sets of ideas in the world, and if we further accept that it is not possible to make theory- or schema-free observational statements, then reality itself cannot influence how we acquire knowledge of it. What this means is that there may be a number of different ways of knowing the world and no means of distinguishing between them. Foundationalists think otherwise.

Classical or demonstrative conceptions of foundationalism maintain that any justification for the truth of an educational proposition rests on identifying those basic principles which underpin subsequent statements about the issue and, more importantly, those inferences that allow the researcher to move from premise to conclusion. These basic principles or beliefs have to be self-evident, which means that they do not require any further justification. Williams (2001) suggests that epistemic foundationalism has two forms. The first of these is structural and he argues that this is where beliefs are said to be basic when there is no need for further evidence to justify them, or those beliefs are inferentially connected to basic or self-evident beliefs which do not require any further justification. The second form of epistemic foundationalism developed by Williams (2001) is what he calls substantive foundationalism. This has all the characteristics of structural foundationalism, and in addition, is epistemically basic, because such beliefs are 'intrinsically credible or self-evidencing' (Williams, 2001, p. 201). What this means is that it plays the end role in any chain of justification, and there is nowhere else to go if such a justification is sought. These beliefs then, if they can be identified, are sufficient for framing the contents and processes that constitute a curriculum.

A number of foundationalist justifications for the inclusion of items and processes in a curriculum have been developed. The first of these we might want to designate as broadly philosophical, and this is where logical delineations between domains of knowledge can be identified. Each of these domains has distinctive kinds of concepts, and distinctive ways of determining truth from falsehood (cf. Hirst, 1972). A second justification for inclusion of items in a curriculum and the exclusion of others is broadly psychological: individual learners have cognitive or mental capacities which are separate and act separately from other mental capacities. Furthermore, individuals have been shown to differ in their capacity to perform these different types of operations (cf. Gardner, 1983). A third set of justifications moves us out of the mind and focuses on the culture we inhabit. All functioning societies have similar sets of knowledge delineations, where these delineations refer to activities in societies, and therefore because they are universal, the argument is that they should be represented in the curriculum (cf. Lawton, 1989). A fourth type of curriculum justification locates the curriculum in natural processes of progression. A child, unless they are restricted in some way, will inherently grow as a conscious being, and this is not dependent on the way society is structured or arranged. The epistemological claims made for each type of justification are not accepted by post-positivist philosophers (cf., for example, Bhaskar, 2010; Brandom, 2000; Haack, 2008) in that they imply an essentialist view of knowledge and its divisions and a neglect of the transitivity inherent in the development of knowledge within the disciplines.

Instrumentalism

A different type of justification for the inclusion of items in a curriculum rejects foundationalist justifications, and suggests that any justification for the contents of a curriculum has to rest with some conception of what one is trying to achieve in the delivery of that curriculum. As a result children in formal education, having been through a process of successful exposure to this curriculum, are acquainted with certain designated types of knowledge, have developed certain designated skills, and have acquired certain designated dispositions, which, it is argued, allow them to lead a fulfilled life, and which also allow everyone else within that society to lead a fulfilled life. This justification is clearly normative and instrumental. What this implies is that a set of experiences can be identified which a child is exposed to and that these lead inexorably to the development of knowledge constructs, skills and dispositions which can be utilised by the individual outside of (in time and place) the learning environment. There are two principal problems with this approach: it is difficult to identify and reach agreement about what the good life for all is, or at least a life for all which allows everyone to be fulfilled; and there is an equal difficulty with identifying experiences for children in school which will lead to the development of knowledge constructs, skills and dispositions so as to allow the individual to lead a fulfilled life when they leave school (cf. Reiss & White, 2012).

A variety of instrumentalist curriculum rationales have been developed, such as autonomous instrumentalism, critical instrumentalism and economic instrumentalism. Instrumentalism denotes a view of the curriculum that makes reference to a future state of affairs for the learner which is external to the setting in which the learning is taking place. Autonomous instrumentalism refers to a view of the curriculum in which pedagogic arrangements, knowledge or skill orientations, knowledge framing, relations between knowledge domains, progression and pacing in the learning environment, relations between the teacher and learner, relations between types of learners, spatial and temporal arrangements and criteria for evaluation are determined by the principle that the end-product is an autonomous individual, or at least an individual who is able to exercise their autonomy, even if they choose not to or are prevented from doing so. Critical instrumentalism, in contrast, as a rationale for a curriculum and its internal relations, seeks to eliminate from society sources of inequality and unfairness. The purpose is therefore indubitably normative. Economic forms of instrumentalism prioritise the economic over other functions in society (see, for example, California Career Technical Education Model Curriculum Standards, 2006).

These different versions of instrumentalism, though rooted in different value-systems and educational rationales, have a similar form. There are three stages in their formation. A preferred vision of society and the conditions for the existence of such a society are identified. The role and purposes of the education system, and the contents and form that a curriculum should take to realise these ends, are clarified, and finally, after the most effective means for the delivery of those ends have been identified, they are enacted, resulting in changes to existing curricular forms and subsequently to changes in society. Young (2005) suggests that instrumentalist forms of knowledge suffer from the external fallacy, where knowledge is treated as provisional, contingent and arbitrary, and curricular knowledge is identified exclusively in terms of specific social goals.

Pragmatic arguments

A further rationale for the curriculum is provided by those who subscribe to pragmatist philosophies, an epistemic version of which has come to be known as inferentialism. Derry (2013, p. 232) suggests that:

> the gist of the argument is that in order to make a claim of knowing we are not, as commonly thought, giving a description of an event but placing our claims about it in a space of reasons – that is to say, making claims on the basis of knowing what follows from them and what it is necessary to assume in order to make them in the first place. Where a word is used without the user being aware of its conceptual connections to other concepts, these connections are still present.

This places knowledge within networks of meaning that are social in character and historical in origin.

There are a number of other curriculum ideologies which broadly can be thought of as pragmatic (in a philosophical sense). Peirce's (1982) pragmatic maxim was that any theory of meaning takes as axiomatic that the content of a proposition is the experienced difference between it being true or false. Truth is therefore understood in terms of the practical effects of what is believed, and particularly, how useful it is. The concept of usefulness is and can be used in a number of different ways, that is, making a set of propositions more coherent or consistent, or alleviating some need in the world, or fulfilling a personal desire, or moving from one state to another.

A further version of pragmatism is that something is true if it enables that person to say that this mechanism or sequence of activities will happen or can be sustained in other situations than those in which it is being applied. It therefore has an external validity dimension. This points to the idea that something is true if it works, and this immediately presents itself as problematic because a further justification needs to be provided as to whether what works is ethically sound or has consequences that can be judged to be ethically sound. Furthermore, any theory which incorporates an external validity element is realist in principle, even if this begs the question as to what type of realism is being advocated.

A final pragmatic justification then is that a rationale for including an item in a curriculum and excluding another rests on the consequences of it becoming a part of that curriculum and on how that curriculum plays out in practice; so a judgement is made between two different items on the grounds that one is more likely to be useful than the other. We should note the way that an epistemic judgement (in the traditional sense, and where this refers to a true or false proposition) is being replaced by a pragmatic judgement about efficacy, though in this case a different type of truth theory is being invoked. As a result, it is possible to argue that an item should be included in the curriculum because it is more practically adequate, that is, human practices within which it is subsumed work in a better way as a result of its inclusion. The issue still remains as to what might constitute successful work, or, to put it another way, what criteria can be used to judge whether the practical adequacy of one practice is superior to another. This can only be resolved by arguing that one theory contributes to a better way of life than the other, and that this better way of life is determined by preferences of people in society and instantiated through current networks of power. The problem with this is that those sets of indicators which determine whether a theory is practically adequate may not be accepted by those who hold a different and rival theory, and thus this cannot form a basis for distinguishing between different theories except in so far as this is decided on the basis of asymmetrical power arrangements within society. Even here it is not possible to say with any certainty that one is more practically adequate than another as a result of current arrangements in society, because what those arrangements signify might be disputed, and, in addition, they are likely to change over time. Pragmatists foreground the social in knowledge-production and it is therefore important to examine social theories of knowledge, whilst also avoiding some of the problems inherent in these epistemologies.

Social epistemologies

A number of social epistemologies have been developed: social constructivism, social realism, epistemic realism, inferentialism and critical realism. The first of these is social constructivism. In opposition to a belief in a mind-independent reality, strong social constructivists avoid epistemic commitments, and locate justificationary rationales, and apparatus in specific discursive formations, which cannot be externally referenced. The argument being made then is that all truth claims emanate from agreements or disagreements between human beings in the present and stretching back in time, which can be and have been only resolved by the exercise of power in society. Thus, gradations of knowledge, where one form is considered to be more true, more adequate or more reliable than another, are not accepted, nor are knowledge constructs which are legitimised by reference to metaphysics, rationality, logic, essentialism or even intuition. Knowledge is the result of struggles in the past about the means for distinguishing true from false statements, and in the sense that the contingencies of history resulted in one such mechanism enduring at the expense of its rivals, knowledge comes into being. This social epistemology is generally challenged on the grounds that the issues surrounding epistemic relativism are not resolved in a satisfactory way (see, for example, Cromby & Nightingale, 1999).

A second framework is social realism. This is a philosophy developed in reaction to the excesses of social constructivism, and in particular, its irrealist assumptions. It parts company with social constructivism by its insistence that it is the social nature of knowledge (and this includes the way it is constructed, developed, given the status of theoretical knowledge, etc.) which allows theorists to make the claim that knowledge is legitimate (cf. Young, 2005). As a result, though knowledge has a social basis, this does not mean that it is being reduced to vested interests, the activities of specific issue groups, or even relations of power. Even if one accepts that knowledge production is not tied inexorably to the furtherance of particular vested interests, including the furtherance of cognitive interests, this does not mean that there is no room for cognitive values which are independent of local power struggles, or that there are no cognitive values relative to particular places and times or specific discourse communities, or that there are no means for determining that a particular curriculum is better than another, or even that there is no infrastructure for the production of knowledge which transcends time and place. The sociality of knowledge therefore does not undermine its objectivity, but is a necessary condition for that objectivity to be realised. Furthermore, if this view is correct, then knowledge processes such as differentiation, fragmentation, subsumption, progression and the like are key moments in its development, and thus key framing devices for understanding it and its legitimation.

However, what is central to this as a curriculum rationale is a belief that some knowledge is objective (and therefore should be included in the curriculum) in ways that transcend the historical conditions of its production. And this in turns means that it has to be possible to distinguish between those elements of knowledge which have been formed as a result of struggles within disciplines about legitimacy and form and those which have not emerged in this way. This would seem to be impossible to achieve for practical reasons, and even then other curriculum rationales would need to be invoked, such as instrumentalist, epistemic or pragmatic justifications.

A version of this argument can be developed from a particular reading of the Russian psychologist, Lev Vygotsky. He distinguishes between thinking and sensation, or science and common sense. What is being suggested here is that higher levels of thinking or of how we can respond to the environment have been developed within the disciplines, and these have been characterised as science. This form of knowledge can be contrasted with common sense forms of knowledge. It is:

> not only a transition from matter that is incapable of sensation to matter that is capable of sensation, but a transition of sensation to thought. This implies that reality is reflected in consciousness in a qualitatively different way in thinking than it is in immediate sensation. (Vygotsky, 1987, p. 47)

We should note here that this viewpoint privileges thought over sensation without saying why it is more important, even though the suggestion is that without thought an aspect of consciousness is neglected. What this argument is suggesting is that it is possible to identify a transcendental condition for the production of knowledge and the form that it should take. However, this transcendental condition necessarily has pragmatic and normative elements in the way it is constituted, and therefore there would need to be an acknowledgement of these in providing a rationale for a curriculum.

A third position, epistemic realism, is qualitatively different. As Putnam (2004) has suggested, our conceptual frameworks, perspectives on the world and descriptive languages interpenetrate what we are calling reality to such an extent that it is impossible to conceive of a pre-schematised world. However, this has a number of consequences and difficulties for an exclusively representational view of knowledge; so for example, the curriculum cannot be a simple representation (expressed as a series of facts) of what is out there in the world because the world is not entirely separate from those mediating devices that human beings have developed to make sense of it, and this therefore means that in order to develop a curriculum rationale we have to take account of those activities which we might want to call epistemic-to-ontic (i.e. knowledge of the world to being in the world) and ontic-to-epistemic (i.e. being in the world to knowledge of it) transactions. This has certain implications. The first of these is that a correspondence between a static intransitive world and an unchanging epistemic world misrepresents the nature of both and the relationship between them. Second, any attempt at describing the world always has the potentiality to change it, though not in every circumstance. Third, regardless of the accuracy or authenticity of the original set of descriptors, and as a result of this epistemic-to-ontic activity, those descriptors may become more accurate or more authentic. Though this suggests a one-way relationship, this is misleading. Those conceptual framings and sets of descriptors are informed, constrained and enabled in a non-trivial way by the world or reality at the particular moment in time in which they are being used, and in turn the shape and form of the ontological realm is influenced by the types of knowledge that are developed.

Representational epistemologies in some of their manifestations construe knowledge as a collection of social facts. Some social facts are facts by virtue of an agreement by people to act as though they exist, for example, fixed and differential intelligences (see Dweck, 2007, for a refutation), or dyslexia (see Hacking, 2000, again for a refutation); in this case, that agreement is forged in the present and deliberately so. Social facts are facts by virtue of an agreement which has evolved over time, are likely to have been created within disciplines or practices of knowledge-making, and users may have forgotten that they were constructed, created or invented in the past, so deeply embedded into the collective psyche have they become. (For an example of a curriculum that has adopted this curricular form, see the new History Programme of Study for England, 2013.)

Brandom (2000) has argued against a representational mode of knowledge, so that knowledge which is considered to be legitimate can be said to be discourse-specific, and prioritising of parts of that discourse: a particular speech act and an associated language game. The speech act is that of asserting and the language game which he privileges is the giving and asking for reasons. As Derry (2013, p. 231) suggests, this has significant implications for pedagogy:

> However, though word meaning may be tightly connected with its referent, how this connection arises is a matter of significant pedagogical importance. For, in the light of Brandom's *inferentialism*, we can understand the forging of the connection between word and object as one that involves reversing the conceptual framework in which so much conventional pedagogical practice operates. Instead the emphasis needs to be on bringing the learner into the inferential relations that constitute a concept prior to its acquisition.

An inferentialist approach to knowledge development and to understanding what knowledge is also has implications for those processes of evaluation, assessment, attribution and normalisation which are central to any constructions of a curriculum.

A final theory of knowledge and therefore of learning and one which understands it as the principal activity of consciousness is provided by the philosophy of critical realism. Critical realists make three claims: there are significant differences between the transitive realm of knowing and the intransitive realm of being; the social world is an open system, and reality has ontological depth. The first of these is that a distinction is made between the intransitive world of being and the transitive world of knowing, with the consequence that if they are conflated, either upwards, resulting in the epistemic fallacy, or downwards, resulting in the ontic fallacy, some meaning is lost (cf. Bhaskar, 2010). This suggests that the transitive and intransitive realms may become disconnected. The second claim made by critical realists is that the social world is an open system, in which objects have emergent properties. Closed systems are characterised by two conditions: objects operate in consistent ways, and they do not change their essential nature. Neither of these conditions operates in open systems.

The third claim is that social reality has ontological depth. Social objects are the real manifestations of the idealised types used in discourses. They are structured in different ways, and because of this, they possess powers. The powers that these structures exert can be manifested in three ways: they can be possessed, exercised or actualised (cf. Brown, Fleetwood & Roberts, 2002). Powers that are possessed are powers that objects have whether they are triggered by the circumstances or not, and they may not be directly observable. Powers that are exercised have been triggered and are having an effect in an open system, and as a result they are interacting with other powers of other structures. These powers may still not be directly observable as other powers of other structures may be acting against them. Powers that have been actualised are generating their effects; so that within the open system they are working together with other powers, but in this case they have not been suppressed or counteracted. Embodied, institutional or discursive structures can be possessed and not exercised or actualised, possessed and exercised, or possessed and actualised. As a result, a causal model based on constant conjunctions is rejected and replaced by a generative-productive one, and objects and relations between objects have emergent properties.

Knowledge-development is not understood in essentialist or metaphysical terms, whether this refers to subjectivity, agency, mind, structures or even the social, nor is the theory of mind which underpins it. However, critical realism is an indirect realist theory and therefore employs processes of modelling and retroduction to provide accounts of knowledge-development practices and the relations between them over time.

Concluding thoughts

The argument being made here has sought to provide a justification for knowledge as the central dimension of the curriculum. Two types of justification were invoked to support this. The first was to conceptualise learning as an epistemic activity, and the second was to suggest that those curriculum ideologies which marginalise knowledge are deficient in some way or another. It then became necessary to determine what this knowledge is, and again there was a need to distinguish it from those curriculum ideologies which purport to prioritise knowledge but which produce in the end distorted versions of it. Three overarching epistemic frameworks were examined: foundationalism, instrumentalism and pragmatism, and each in turn was criticised for an excessive focus in the first case on an essentialist view of knowledge and its divisions and a neglect of the transitivity inherent in the development of knowledge within the disciplines; in the second case on knowledge being treated as provisional, contingent and arbitrary, and curricular knowledge being identified exclusively in terms of specific social goals; and in the third case, on the social basis of knowledge-development and learning, without at the same time providing any transcendental grounding of knowledge in reality.

These viewpoints point to the need to foreground the social in any curriculum rationale and in understanding this fundamental element, five social epistemologies were examined: social constructivism, social realism, epistemic realism, inferentialism and critical realism. Elements taken from each allow one to develop a way of determining what should be included in and what should be excluded from a curriculum. Thus the principles from which a curriculum rationale can be developed are as follows:

- There is a social dimension to knowledge-construction, but this does not categorically preclude reference to a world which is separate from the way it is being described.
- Conceptual framings and sets of descriptors are informed, constrained and enabled in a non-trivial way by the world or reality at the particular moment in time in which they are being used, and in turn the shape and form of the ontological realm is influenced by the types of knowledge that are being developed.
- Our conceptual frameworks, perspectives on the world and descriptive languages interpenetrate what we are calling reality to such an extent that it is impossible to conceive of a pre-schematised world. However, this does not preclude indirectly conceived references to the structures of the world.
- A curriculum cannot be a simple representation (expressed as a series of facts) of what is out there in the world because the world is not entirely separate from those mediating devices that human beings have developed to make sense of it.
- It is important to avoid essentialising knowledge and its divisions and neglecting the transitivity inherent in the development of knowledge within the disciplines.
- Any knowledge claim has to be placed within the space of reasons, which means that this claim is discourse-specific and positioned within conceptual frameworks that precede it in time and place and have implications for future use.

- There are significant differences between the transitive realm of knowing and the intransitive realm of being; the social world is an open system; and reality has ontological depth.
- It is possible to identify a transcendental condition for the production of knowledge and the form that it should take. However, this transcendental condition necessarily has pragmatic and normative elements in the way it is constituted, and therefore there would need to be an acknowledgement of these in providing a rationale for a curriculum.

Translating these knowledge constructs into practical forms of curriculum development is the next step. The issues then of how knowledge is transformed at the pedagogic and evaluative sites, and the relationship between these three sites, are important, even though the arguments for them are undeveloped here. However, what it is possible to suggest is that those relations between curriculum contents, pedagogic forms, evaluative processes and criteria are a function of how knowledge is conceived and used within a curriculum, rather than they being independently derived.

References

Bhaskar, R. (2010). *Reclaiming reality*. London: Routledge.
Brandom, R. (2000). *Articulating reasons: An introduction to inferentialism*. Cambridge, MA: Harvard University Press.
Brown, A., Fleetwood, S., & Roberts, J. (2002). *Critical realism and marxism*. London: Routledge.
California Career Technical Education Model Curriculum Standards: Grades Seven through Twelve. (2006). Sacramento, CA: California State Board of Education.
Cromby, J., & Nightingale, D. (1999). What's wrong with social constructionism? In D. Nightingale & J. Cromby (Eds.), *Social constructionist psychology: A critical analysis of theory and practice* (p. 35). Buckingham: Open University Press.
Derry, J. (2013). Can inferentialism contribute to social epistemology. *Journal of Philosophy of Education, 47*(2), 222–235.
Dweck, C. (2007). *Mindset: The new psychology of success*. New York, NY: Ballantine Books.
Gardner, H. (1983). *Frames of mind*. New York, NY: Basic Books.

Haack, S. (2008). *Putting philosophy to work: Inquiry and its place in culture*. London: Prometheus Books.

Hacking, I. (2000). *The social construction of what?* Harvard, MA: Harvard University Press.

Hirst, P. (1972). Liberal education and nature of knowledge. In R. Dearden, P. Hirst, & R. Peters (Eds.), *Education and reason: Part three of education and the development of reason*. London: Routledge and Kegan Paul.

Lawton, D. (1989). *Education, culture and the national curriculum*. London: Hodder and Stoughton.

History Programme of Study for England. (2013). London: Department of Education.

Organisation for Economic Cooperation and Development. (2009). *Knowledge and skills for life: PISA*. Paris: Author.

Peirce, C. S. (1982). Pragmatics. In N. Houser, C. Kloesel, & the Peirce Edition Project (Eds.), *The essential Peirce* (2 Vols., pp. 134 179) Bloomington, IN: Indiana University Press.

Putnam, H. (2004). *The collapse of the fact/value dichotomy and other essays*. Cambridge, MA: Harvard University Press.

Reiss, M., & White, J. (2012). *An aims-based curriculum: The significance of human flourishing for schools (Bedford Way paper)*. London: Institute of Education Press.

Sellars, W. (1997). *Empiricism and the philosophy of mind*. Cambridge, MA: Harvard University Press.

Vygotsky, L. S. (1987). Mind in society. In R. Reiber & A. S. Carton (Eds.), *The collected works of L. S. Vygotsky* (Vol. 1, pp. 1 132). New York, NY: Plenum Press.

White, J. (1982). *The aims of education revisited*. London: Routledge and Kegan Paul.

Williams, M. (2001). *Problems of knowledge: A critical introduction to epistemology*. Oxford: Oxford University Press.

Young, M. (2005). *Bringing knowledge back in: From social constructivism to social realism in the sociology of education*. London: Routledge.

Pragmatising the curriculum: bringing knowledge back into the curriculum conversation, but via pragmatism

Gert Biesta

Faculty of Language and Literature, Humanities, Arts and Education, Institute of Education and Society, University of Luxembourg, Walferdange, Luxembourg

> In this paper, I explore the role of knowledge in the curriculum through a discussion of John Dewey's transactional theory of knowing. I do so against the background of recent calls to bring knowledge back into the discussion about the curriculum in which pragmatism has been depicted as a problematic form of relativism that should have no place in contemporary curriculum theory and practice. I show that rather than being a form of relativism, pragmatism actually moves beyond the modern opposition of objectivism versus relativism. Dewey's transactional theory of knowing moves the question of knowledge from the domain of certainty to the domain of possibility. I show in this paper how Dewey develops this argument and give reasons why this is an important contribution to the ongoing discussion about knowledge and the curriculum.

Introduction: bringing knowledge back in

In a number of recent publications, the British sociologist Michael Young has argued that there is a need to bring knowledge back into the discussion about the curriculum (for example, Young, 2008; see also Balarin, 2008; Young & Muller, 2007, 2008). I agree with Young that the question of knowledge may indeed have disappeared from parts of curriculum theory and parts of curriculum practice. This is partly the result of a phenomenon to which I have referred as the 'learnification' of education (see Biesta, 2010a). 'Learnification' refers to a fairly recent development in which the language of education has been taken over by a language of learning. As a result, the emphasis in the discussion has shifted from questions about the content of education to questions about process, for example, in the now ubiquitous idea of 'learning to learn' or in the influence that so-called '21st skills' are having on curricula in many countries (see http://www.p21.org; and for a more detailed discussion of this trend Biesta, 2013b). Discussions about knowledge thus seem to have been sidelined in favour of discussions about skills and competences. Young and colleagues have sought to bring knowledge back into the conversation by taking recourse to social realism (see particularly Young, 2008). Social realism is presented as an alternative to forms of social constructivism which, according to Young, are not only unable to account for 'the idea of knowledge growth' but also encourage 'students and educational researchers to neglect the "realist" traditions of social theory' (Young & Muller, 2008, p. 521). Pragmatism – mainly read through the eyes of Durkheim (see Young, 2008) – is one of the forms of social constructivism which, according to Young, suffers from these problems and therefore needs to be replaced or overcome (see, for example, Young, 2008, pp. 80, 145).

With his critique of pragmatism Young is part of a much longer line of authors who all have suggested that pragmatism is a form of anti-realist philosophy with strong relativist tendencies and implications (for example, Horkheimer, 1947). In this paper, I wish to argue that rather than being anti-realist and relativistic, pragmatism actually operates *beyond* the age-old opposition of objectivism and relativism (see also Bernstein, 1983). It is for this reason that I believe that pragmatism – and particularly the pragmatism developed by John Dewey – still has important insights to offer for the discussion about knowledge and the curriculum, so that, rather than casting it aside as being part of the problem, it should actually be (re)considered as a productive way for engaging with the question of knowledge in the curriculum conversation.[1]

Knowledge and the curriculum

Early on in his career, the American philosopher and educationalist John Dewey stated that the problem of education lies in the co-ordination of the individual and the social factors (Dewey, 1895[2]). The idea of co-ordination remained a central theme in Dewey's work, as can be seen from book titles such as *The School and Society* (1899), *The Child and the Curriculum* (1902), *Democracy and Education* (1916), and *Experience and Education* (1938). The appearance of the word 'and' in the title of many of Dewey's books signifies that he was wary of one-sided thinking that would put the emphasis either on the school *or* on society, either on the child *or* on the curriculum, either on experience *or* on education, and so on. This already reveals that a common characterisation of Dewey's position as being a child-centred conception of education clearly misrepresents his ideas. Elsewhere (Biesta, 2006), I have suggested to refer to Dewey's position as a *communication-centred* view of education, arguing that what matters for Dewey is the connection, that which happens 'in between' – or with a more technical term he introduced towards the end of his career: *transaction* (Dewey & Bentley, 1949; see also Biesta & Burbules, 2003). For Dewey, education is neither about getting the curriculum into the child nor about the child just doing anything, but about establishing a productive and meaningful connection between the two.

From the angle of pedagogy this idea makes sense, as pedagogy operates precisely in the middle ground between the child and the curriculum. The point of pedagogy, after all, is not to make sure that children learn but that they learn *something* (see also Biesta, 2010a). That is why pedagogy should indeed be focused on the co-ordination of the child and the curriculum. Whereas the idea of co-ordination makes sense from the point of view of pedagogy – that is from the point of view of the *process* of education – it becomes more problematic from the point of view of the *content* of education. How much leeway, so we might ask, should there be for the child to creatively interpret and appropriate the curriculum? Isn't the very point of education that children not just 'get' the curriculum but that they get it 'right'? And doesn't that imply that while there is an obvious need for the co-ordination of the individual and the social factors, ultimately this co-ordination is strongly biased – and has to be strongly biased – towards the curriculum end of the spectrum?

Let us begin by saying that the answer to these questions has to be that it depends. It first of all depends on what one expects from education. Education is, after all, not just a 'machine' for the transmission of knowledge and skills (the domain of qualification), but is involved in wider ambitions, such as the introduction of children into existing traditions and practices (the domain of socialisation), and questions concerning the formation of the person (what elsewhere I have termed 'subjectification' – see Biesta, 2010a). While one may argue that to the extent to which education is focused on the transmission of knowledge and skills, there is an important need for getting it 'right,' to the extent to which education is focused on the formation of the person and on questions of agency and freedom, the idea of getting it 'right' becomes far less meaningful. We also should not forget that 'the curriculum' is itself a multifaceted phenomenon. The requirements for a curriculum for learning mathematics are, after all, quite different from curricula concerned with, for example, car mechanics, aviation, brain surgery, beauty therapy, citizenship, critical thinking, and so on. It is also important not to think of these as entirely separate areas. While there may be an argument for 'getting it right' in a subject like geography, we should also want students to develop a critical understanding of the field, which requires that such a curriculum should always be orientated towards more than just 'getting it right' in the sense of 'getting the facts right'. Similarly, for many practical areas, one could argue that the point is not simply to acquire the right skills, but also to develop the capacity for critical judgement in relation to them – and this is as important for the brain surgeon and the Airbus pilot as it is for the beauty therapist and the car mechanic.

I consider these preliminary remarks quite important for the discussion about knowledge and the curriculum, as they can help us to keep the discussion 'grounded' and focused, and prevent us from making the mistake that we can talk about 'curriculum' and 'knowledge' just in an abstract sense, disconnected from where particular issues arise and problems emerge. This is not to suggest that the discussion is entirely specific and particular, but the challenge is to ask the right questions and identify the real issues. With respect to the question of knowledge this is quite difficult, not in the least because the discussion about knowledge and the curriculum is highly politicised, both from the angle of policy and practice – which, itself, is connected to wider public debates about what education is for – and from the angle of research.

The politics of knowledge

One way to map the increased politicisation of the discussion is by tracing the development from the year 1854 when Herbert Spencer argued that the 'question of all questions' for the development of a 'rational curriculum' had to be 'What knowledge is of most worth?' (Spencer, 1909) – to which, by the way, his answer was 'science' – to the 1980s when Michael Apple rephrased Spencer's question as 'Whose knowledge is of most worth?' (see, for example, Apple, 1991, 1996).[3] Apple thus articulated a *sociological* perspective on knowledge and the curriculum which suggested that, at least from an analytical perspective – that is, from the angle of trying to understand why the curriculum is what it is and does what it does – we should not be asking philosophical questions about the 'intrinsic qualities' of knowledge but should shift to sociological questions that focus on the 'extrinsic connections' of the curriculum. This, as said, was partly meant to understand the curriculum and its workings – and in this regard it was supported by historical studies of the curriculum that had a similar outlook (for example, Kliebard, 1987) – although it was informed by the wider ambition that the sociological exposure of the workings of power could open up opportunities for different knowledges and different constituencies to populate the curriculum, and thus benefit from its power. In North America, this almost seamlessly fed into much bigger 'culture wars' that led to the hyper-politicisation of discussions about culture, knowledge, and the curriculum – discussions that are still very much part of the political landscape today. In Britain, not surprisingly, the discussion about knowledge and the curriculum mapped far less onto race, gender, and religion – to name a number of the key 'markers' of the 'culture wars' – but focused much more on class (see, for example, Bernstein, 1971).

The way in which the discussion about knowledge and the curriculum has developed, leads to a predicament, if not a paradox. In terms of truth – I will return to the question of knowledge and the relationship between knowledge and truth later – we could say that we find, on the one hand, those who claim the truth for their particular views (and this includes both Spencer and his followers and those who take a particular position within the 'culture wars'), while, on the other hand, the sociology of the curriculum relativises these truth claims by arguing that they all speak from a particular position and all articulate a particular interest. The predicament is that in doing so the sociology of the curriculum expresses a truth claim as well – roughly 'all knowledge is social' or 'all knowledge is relative to social position' or 'all knowledge is socially constructed' – and thus ends up doing the very thing it tries to criticise. This indicates that the favourite strategy of the left – that of speaking truth to power – may not be as easy to deliver as is sometimes assumed. This was the point made by Foucault when he introduced the idea of 'power/knowledge' which, unlike what some of his readers seem to assume, was not to make the sociological point that power is everywhere, but rather to highlight that power and knowledge always come together so that they can no longer speak to each other, so to speak. For Foucault, this did not imply the end of enlightenment, but only the end of a particular (modern) strategy to achieve enlightenment, one based on the alleged separation of knowledge and power (see Foucault, 1984).

Beyond objectivism and relativism: insights from pragmatism

I have spent a considerable amount of words trying to outline some of the issues that are at stake in the discussion about knowledge and the curriculum, so that we do not too quickly start with formulating another answer or articulating another position, but rather try to start from a good enough sense of the problems we are trying to address. Having done so, however, leaves us perhaps a bit empty-handed, as it is not immediately obvious where we can go next. While the sociology of the curriculum has generated important insights about curricular knowledge, it cannot act as the ultimate arbiter on questions of knowledge. The main unease when everything becomes sociologised and when everything is seen as a social construction, is that the idea of knowledge itself begins to disappear, so that we end up with a universe full of opinions (what the Greek philosophers called doxa [δόξα]) but without any truth (in Greek philosophy known as episteme [ἐπιστήμη]). However, I also do not think that we can any longer just turn to philosophy – and more specifically to this subfield of philosophy called epistemology – for an answer, as the idea that philosophy can provide us with a deeper truth about what it means to know and what it means to have knowledge, has also reached its limits. Does that mean, then, that we are forever doomed to bounce back and forth between truth and its impossibility, between objectivism and relativism, between realism and anti-realism, between truths and perspectives, and between the one and the many?

This conclusion, I think, does not make sense at an intuitive level either. There are, after all, situations in which the distinction between truth and falsehood can be quite easily made. There are instances where truth has indeed spoken effectively against power or has been mobilised effectively to do so (think, for example, of the South African Truth and Reconciliation Commission). Also, realism at least seems to be an attractive assumption for leading our everyday lives. While we know that both the social and the natural world are amenable to a wide range of different interpretations, we also know that not any interpretation makes sense. And we know that not everything that we want the world to be or to do is actually possible. We have a lot of technology that seems to be working perfectly well, which seems to give at least some credence to the scientific insights upon which it is supposed to be based – my phrasing is careful here, because there is a question whether technology is indeed *based* upon knowledge and whether the success of technology *proves* anything about the knowledge involved (for more on this, see Biesta, 2011; see also Gellner, 1992 who does suggest that the effectiveness of technology proves the truth of the underlying knowledge; and see Böhme, Van den Daele, Hohlfeld, Krohn, & Schäfer, 1983 for the relationship between development of knowledge and development of technology). And as educators, we should have the ambition to engage in a meaningful and intelligent way with these intuitions in our educational practices.

Could it be, perhaps, that the reason for the clash between our theoretical discussions on the one hand and our everyday intuitions on the other may not so much be the result of us having the wrong answers, but follows from the fact that we may have been asking the wrong questions? And could it perhaps be the case that we have been asking the wrong questions because some of the assumptions from which our questions stem themselves need revision? This is where we should turn to pragmatism – and more specifically the work of John Dewey – because this is precisely the point Dewey has been making throughout his career, that is, that the problem with so many discussions about knowledge is that they articulate different positions within the same set of assumptions rather than trying to break away from those assumptions in order to ask different questions and thus have the prospect of different and perhaps better answers. While I do not have the space to deal with the full detail of Dewey's work,[4] I wish to offer some insights from Dewey's pragmatism in order to show why I think that his ideas (still) matter for contemporary discussions about knowledge and the curriculum. I will present Dewey's ideas in three steps. I will first say a few things about modern epistemology and what I will refer to as the 'mind-world scheme'. I will then give a reconstruction of Dewey's transactional theory of knowing. In the third step, I will outline some implications of Dewey's views, before I return to the wider discussion about knowledge and the curriculum.

Modern epistemology and the 'mind-world scheme'

In modern epistemology, the question of knowledge is often phrased as the question how the human mind can acquire knowledge of a world outside of itself. Robert Nozick put the challenge most succinctly when he asked whether we can ever know that we are *not* a brain suspended in a vat full of liquid, wired to a computer which is feeding our current experiences (see Nozick, 1981, pp. 161–171). Nozick is part of a long tradition in which the nature of knowledge is examined from a *skeptical* point of view, that is by starting from the assumption that knowledge may *not* be possible because we may not be able to get 'outside' of our own mind. The first philosopher to place skepticism at the heart of modern epistemology was René Descartes. In the *Second Meditation* he used the 'method of doubt' to arrive at the conclusion that although we can doubt everything, we cannot, when doing so, doubt that we are engaged in a process of doubting. Whereas this provided Descartes with certainty about the existence of the thinking self, it did *not* provide any certainty about the existence of a world *beyond* our experience, and this issue has troubled modern epistemology ever since. It eventually led David Hume to the conclusion that the existence of an external world of enduring object is a 'very useful hypothesis,' but not something that can ever be proven.

What unites the ideas of Nozick, Descartes, and Hume is their reliance on a dualistic view of reality. They assume that reality consists of two totally different 'substances', mind and matter, and that the question of knowledge has to begin with the mind in order then to ask how the mind can get in touch with the material world 'outside' of itself. The dualism between mind and matter has not only set the agenda for modern epistemology by giving it the task to answer the question how the mind can get 'in touch' with the world (see, for example, Dancy, 1985) – which is one reason why epistemology cannot be a neutral arbiter in discussions about knowledge, as it is itself 'tainted' by very specific assumptions. The dualism between mind and matter has also provided the framework for the distinction between objectivity and subjectivity and, related to this, for distinctions such as between absolutism and relativism, between realism and idealism, etcetera. After all, on the basis of the dualism between knowing subjects and objects to be known, knowledge can be objective if it depicts how objects are in themselves; whereas, if this is considered not to be possible, then the only other option is for knowledge to be subjective, i.e., produced by the activities of the human mind.

The implications of this way of thinking go well beyond 'technical' questions about knowledge. Many recent discussions about culture, ethics, morality, science, rationality, and even Western civilization appear to be informed by the idea that the only choice we have is between the two options presented through the 'mind-world scheme'. More importantly, many participants in these discussions seem to fear that if we give up objectivity, the only thing left is chaos. Bernstein (1983, p. 18) aptly refers to this as the 'Cartesian Anxiety', the idea that *either* there is 'a fixed foundation for our knowledge' *or* we cannot escape 'the forces of darkness that envelop us with madness, with intellectual and moral chaos'.

The mind-world scheme does indeed only offer two options: objectivity and subjectivity. The crucial question, however, is not which option to choose. The far more important question is whether the mind-world scheme is itself inevitable or whether it is possible to think about knowledge and reality in a different way, starting from different assumptions. John Dewey's theory of knowing does precisely this. It offers an understanding of knowing that does *not* start from what he saw as the 'impossible question' as to how 'a knower who is purely individual or "subjective," and whose being is wholly psychical and immaterial ... and a world to be known which is purely universal or "objective," and whose being is wholly mechanical and physical' can ever reach each other (Dewey, 1911, p. 441). Instead, Dewey put forward a framework which starts with *interactions* – or as he later preferred to call it: *transactions* – taking place in nature and in which nature itself is understood as 'a moving whole of interacting parts' (Dewey, 1929, p. 232). This is Dewey's self-confessed 'Copernican turn', in which '(t)he old center was mind', while '(t)he new center is indefinite interactions' (Dewey, 1929, p. 232). The key concept in this Copernican turn is 'experience'.

The transactional theory of knowing

While *transaction* refers to interactions taking place in nature more generally, *experience* refers to the transactions of *living* organisms and their environments. What is distinctive about these transactions is that they constitute a *double* relationship:

> The organism acts in accordance with its own structure, simple or complex, upon its surroundings. As a consequence the changes produced in the environment react upon the organism and its activities. The living creature undergoes, suffers, the consequences of its own behavior. This close connection between doing and suffering or undergoing forms what we call experience. (Dewey, 1920, p. 129)

Experience is therefore the way in which living organisms are implicated in their environment. Contrary to what is suggested in the mind-world scheme, Dewey thus argues that experience is not 'a veil that shuts man off from nature', but rather 'a means of penetrating continually further into the heart of nature' (Dewey, 1925, p. 15).

Dewey saw knowing as the mode of experience that in some way 'supports' action. It is concerned with grasping the *relationship* between our actions and their consequences. It is because of this that knowing can help us to get more control over our actions, at least more than in the case of blind trial and error. It is important to see that 'control' here does not mean complete mastery, but the ability to intelligently plan and direct our actions. This ability is first of all important in those situations in which we are not sure how to act – which is expressed in one of Dewey's definitions of knowing as having to do with 'the transformation of disturbed and unsettled situations into those more controlled and more significant' (Dewey, 1929, p. 236). Knowing is also important in order to achieve more control, a more intelligent approach in the other domains of experience, which is expressed in Dewey's claim that knowing 'facilitates control of objects for purposes of non-cognitive experience' (Dewey, 1929, p. 79).

The framework for Dewey's theory of knowing lies in his theory of action, the outlines of which he developed early on in his career in a landmark paper called 'The Reflex Arc Concept in Psychology' (Dewey, 1896). One way to summarise Dewey's theory of action is to say that it amounts to *a theory of experimental learning* if, that is, we think of learning as the way in which living organisms interactively 'adapt' to their environments (which in itself is a rather truncated conception of learning, of course; on this see Biesta, 2013a). Dewey characterises living organisms – including human organisms – as capable of establishing and maintaining a dynamic coordination with their environment. Through this process, the predispositions – or 'habits' as Dewey preferred to call them – of the organism become more focused and more specific, more attuned to everchanging environing conditions, which is another way of saying that through the tentative, experimental way in which living organisms maintain coordinated transaction with their environment they *learn*. This learning, however, is *not* the acquisition of information about how the world 'out there' is. It is a learning process through which living organisms acquire a complex and flexible set of predispositions-for-action.

On this view, learning is therefore basically a process of trial and error and in one sense this is indeed how Dewey argues that living organisms learn. However, there is a difference between blind trial and error and what Dewey called 'intelligent action'. The difference has to do with the intervention of thinking, which he defines as 'dramatic rehearsal (in imagination) of various competing possible lines of action' (Dewey, 1922, p. 132). The choice for a specific line of action should be understood as 'hitting in imagination upon an object which furnishes an adequate stimulus to the recovery of overt action' (Dewey, 1922, p. 134). Whether this choice will actually lead to coordinated transaction will only become clear when the organism actually acts. This is why thinking can never guarantee that our actions will result in coordinated transactions. However, what it can do is make the process of choosing more intelligent than would be the case with 'blind' trial-and-error.

In Dewey's view, the question of knowledge – or to be more precise: the issue of knowing – arises 'because of the appearance of incompatible factors within the empirical situation. (...) Then opposed responses are provoked which cannot be taken simultaneously in overt action, and which accordingly can be dealt with, whether simultaneously or successively, only after they have been brought into a plan of organized action' (Dewey, 1916, p. 326). The problem here is one of the *meaning* of the situation – and for Dewey 'situation' always refers to organism and environment in transaction. The only way to solve the problem in an *intelligent* manner and not by simple trial-and-error is by means of a systematic inspection of the situation. On the one hand, we need to identify and state the problem. On the other hand, we need to develop suggestions for addressing the problem, for finding a way to act, and hence to find out what the meaning of the situation actually is. While thought or reflection must play an important part in this process, they will, in themselves, not result in knowledge. It is only when action follows, that the value of both the analysis of the problem and the suggested solution can be established. For Dewey, therefore, we need overt action in order to determine the worth and validity of our reflective considerations. Otherwise we have, at most, a hypothesis about the problem and a hypothesis about its possible solution.

This means that in order to get knowledge we need action. However, although action is a necessary condition for knowledge, it is not a sufficient one. We also need thinking or reflection. It is the *combination* of reflection and action which leads to knowledge. From this, it follows that knowing, the acquisition of knowledge, is not something which takes place somewhere deep down inside the human mind. Knowing is itself an activity, it is 'literally something which we do' (Dewey, 1916, p. 367). The meaning which emerges from the restoration of coordinated action is a meaning 'which is contemporaneously aware of meaning something beyond itself' (Dewey, 1906, p. 113). This 'beyond' is not simply present or will not simply become present in the future. It will *only* become present 'through the intervention of an operation' (Dewey, 1906, pp. 113–114), that is, through what we *do*. A potato becomes edible when we cook it, so after the intervention of the act of cooking – and perhaps we can say: after the discovery that when we cook potatoes we can eat them – the potato means something different in our field of action – it has become 'potentially edible food'. Therefore, when experience is 'cognitional', as Dewey puts it, it means that we perceive something as meaning-something-else-which-we-will-experience-when-we-act-in-a-specific-way. It is along these lines that knowledge is intimately connected to the possibility of control. 'In knowledge', Dewey argued, 'causes become means and effects become consequences, and thereby things having meaning' (Dewey, 1929, p. 236). Knowledge has, in other words, to do with *inference*: a reaction to something which is distant in time or place. Because inference is a step into an unknown future, it is a precarious journey. Inference always involves uncertainty and risk. A stone, Dewey argued, can only react to stimuli of the present, not of the future, and for that reason cannot make mistakes. Since inference entails the possibility of mistake, it introduces truth and falsity into the world.

Experience, reality and knowledge

One important implication of Dewey's transactional definition of experience is that it puts an end to the idea that it is only through knowledge that we can obtain a hold on reality. For Dewey, all modes of experience are equally real, since they are all modes of the transaction of living organisms and their environments. From this, Dewey concluded that 'things – anything, everything, in the ordinary or non-technical use of the term "thing" – are what they are experienced as' (Dewey, 1905, p. 158). This first of all means that everyone's experience is equally real. It also implies that what is experienced is itself real. If someone is frightened by a noise, so Dewey's argument is, then that noise *is* fearsome. This claim must be understood transactionally. If someone is frightened by a sound, then the fear is the immediate response of the organism. The sound *is* frightening because the organism reacts to the sound as being-a-frightening-sound. This implies, however, that *being*-frightened is not the same as knowing-that-one-is-frightened. Knowing what *caused* the fearsome noise is a different experience. While the latter experience may be *more true* than the former, it is in Dewey's view not more *real*. 'The question of truth is not as to whether Being or Non-Being, Reality or mere Appearance is experienced, but as to the *worth* of a certain concretely experienced thing' (Dewey, 1905, p. 163). One important implication of this is that experience in itself does not provide us with any knowledge. Dewey rejected, in other words, the view that experience provides us with elementary 'bits' of knowledge which, when put together in a systematic of logical manner, result in knowledge.[5]

For Dewey, the difference between experience and knowledge is that knowledge is concerned with the *occurrence* of experience. The 'office' of knowledge signifies a search 'for those relations upon which the *occurrence* of real qualities and values depends' (Dewey, 1929, p. 83). In this respect, knowledge is intimately and necessarily connected with action, because – and this is the most crucial point in Dewey's theory of knowing – the discovery of the conditions and consequences of experience 'can take place *only* by modifying the given qualities in such ways that *relations* become manifest' (Dewey 1929, p. 84; emphasis added). The shift from understanding knowledge as being concerned with the world 'as it is' to understanding knowledge as being concerned with *conditions and consequences*, is a very important element of Dewey's approach. It represents a shift from a concern with things as they are to a concern with 'the history to which a given thing belongs' (Dewey, 1925, p. 243). It is a shift from 'knowing as an aesthetic enjoyment of the properties of nature as a world of divine art, to knowing as a means of secular control – that is, a method of purposefully introducing changes which will alter the direction of the course of events' (Dewey, 1929, p. 81). This implies that for Dewey knowledge is concerned with the relations between actions and consequences. This introduces the dimension of *time* into Dewey's theory of knowing – a reason for arguing that Dewey has a temporal conception of knowing.

Dewey's approach also has implications for how we understand the objects of knowledge. Whereas in the dualistic approach the objects of knowledge are seen as 'things' that exist in a world 'out there' and are there for us to discover and depict, Dewey's transactional view sees the objects of knowledge as the *outcomes* of processes of inquiry. Since the habits we acquire through such processes provide us with more specific predispositions for action, habits in a sense embody the ways in which our environment becomes more meaningful for us. The experimental transformation of organism–environment transactions transforms the environment in which and through which we act into what Dewey referred to as 'a figured framework of objects' (Dewey, 1922, p. 128). This is the reason why Dewey referred to objects of perception not as things but as 'events with meaning' (Dewey, 1925, p. 240). In the case of spoken language, it is relatively easy to see that words – or 'sound-events' do not have a meaning of their own, but that they have *become* meaningful over time. It is far more difficult to draw the same conclusion with respect to physical objects, such as chairs, tables, trees, stones, hills and flowers, 'where it seems as if the union of intellectual meaning with physical fact were aboriginal' (Dewey, 1933, p. 231). However, chairs and tables are as much events with meaning as words are (for a similar line of thought see Bloor, 1983, in his discussion of Wittgenstein's social theory of knowledge). And their meaning has a strictly transactional origin, in that it has to be understood as the outcome of the specific ways in which successful relationship between our actions and their consequences have been established over time. It is not, therefore, that through a process of inquiry we can find out what the possible meanings of, for example, a chair are. Rather, a chair specifies a particular way in which the transaction with the environment has become meaningful. It is for this reason that Dewey argued that we should think of objects as tools. 'The character of an object is like that of a tool [...]; it is an order of determination of sequential changes terminating in a foreseen consequence'. (Dewey, 1925, p. 121).[6]

The final element of Dewey's theory of knowing has to do with the question of truth. We have already seen that for Dewey there is no sense in asking about the truth of our immediate experience. Immediate experience simply is what it is. Truth and falsity only enter the scene when we raise questions about the *meaning* of experience. 'Truth and falsity are not properties of any experience or thing, in and of itself or in its first intention; but of things where the problem of assurance consciously enters in. Truth and falsity present themselves as significant facts only in situations in which specific meanings are intentionally compared and contrasted with reference to the question of worth, as to the reliability of meaning' (Dewey, 1906, p. 118; emphasis in original). Truth and falsity are therefore not concerned with things as such, but with the *relationship* between our experience of a thing on the one hand and our possible actions or responses on the other. This not only means that 'truth' is always contextual and related to action. It also means that truth is itself *temporal*. Truth does not refer to an alleged correspondence between a proposition and reality. It has to do with the correspondence between *suggested* meaning and *realised* meaning, that is, meaning 'put into practice'. 'The agreement, correspondence, is between purpose, plan, and its own execution, fulfilment' (Dewey, 1907, p. 84).

This does not mean that truth becomes disconnected from reality. The contrary is the case, not only because of the transactional framework that informs Dewey's theory of knowing but also because of the *indispensable* role of action in the process that results in knowledge. The upshot of this is that knowledge is not a passive registration of reality 'out there'. Our intervention, our action, is a crucial, necessary and constitutive part of knowledge. In this sense, we can say that knowledge is always a human construction just as the objects of knowledge are. However, it does *not* mean that anything is possible. We always intervene in an existing course of events and although our intervention introduces change, it will always be change of an existing course of events. We cannot create out of nothing. For Dewey, the only possible construction is a *re*construction.

Consequences of pragmatism

One of the most important implications of Dewey's transactional approach is that knowledge does *not* provide us with a picture of reality as it is in itself – an idea to which Dewey referred as the 'spectator theory of knowledge'. For Dewey, knowledge always concerns the *relationship* between (our) actions and (their) consequences. This, in essence, is what a transactional conception of knowledge implies. It means that knowledge is a construction or, to be more precise, that the objects of knowledge are constructions. However, contrary to how constructivism is often understood under the mind-world scheme (viz., as purely mental and hence subjective), Dewey's constructivism is a *transactional* constructivism, a constructivism which holds that knowledge is at the very same time constructed *and* real. This is why we can call Dewey's position a form of realism, albeit *transactional realism* (Sleeper, 1986).

Given that knowledge concerns the relationship between (our) actions and (their) consequences, knowledge will only ever offer us *possibilities* but not certainty. The conclusions we draw on the basis of careful observation of what follows from how we act upon the world, show what has been possible in this particular transactional situation. Sometimes what was possible in one situation turns out also to be possible in another situation; but in other situations the transactional determinants of the situation are different, so that what was possible in one case is no longer possible in another case (see also Biesta, 2007 on the implications of this idea for the discussion about 'what works'). This is why Dewey preferred to refer to the outcomes of inquiry and research as 'warranted assertions' rather than truth. The assertions we make about the consequences of our actions are warranted on the basis of careful observation and control. However, they are only warranted in relation to the particular situation in which they were 'produced' and we should not make the mistake – for example by putting the label 'true' on them – to think that they will be warranted for all time and all similar situations. This does not mean that conclusions from one situation cannot be useful for other situations. However, the way in which knowledge from one situation transfers to another situation is in that it can guide our observation and perception and can suggest possible ways for resolving problems, for finding ways forward. Whether these possibilities will address the specific problems in the specific, new transactional situation can only be discovered when we act.

A more general feature of Dewey's transactional approach to knowing is that, contrary to mainstream modern philosophy, his approach is not a sceptical one. For Dewey, there is no gap between human beings and the world. This does not mean that everything we experience is simply 'true'. While Dewey does hold that things are what they are experienced as, there is a crucial difference between experience and knowledge. While experience simply 'is', knowledge, because it has to do with inference, can always be fallible. In this respect, we have to conclude that Dewey's transactional theory of knowing is a form of fallibilism. However, it is important to see that for Dewey knowledge is *not* fallible because of an alleged gap between ourselves and the world, but because we can never be sure what the future will bring, not in the least because what the future will look like depends also on our own ongoing actions. According to the transactional approach, we are not spectators of a finished universe, but participants in an ever-evolving, unfinished universe.

Dewey's transactional approach also cuts across the either/or of objectivism and subjectivism. From a transactional point of view, 'the world' always appears as a function of what we do. Objectivity, understood as a depiction of a world completely independent from and untouched by us, is therefore simply impossible. If we want to know the world, we *must* interact and, as a result, we will only know the world in the way in which it responds to us. The world we construct emerges out of the doing-undergoing-doing dynamics of what Dewey calls 'experience'. One could argue – and many critics of Dewey had done so – that although Dewey rejects objectivism, he thus ends up in a situation of complete subjectivism. Dewey simply acknowledges that this is the case – but he adds that there is no problem with this at all, as long as we see that the worlds we construct are constructed for our own individual purposes, for our own attempts to address the problems we are faced with. It is only when we start to interact with others that the need for some form of coordination of our subjective worlds with the subjective worlds of others arises. What happens in this case is that, through interaction, co-operation, coordination, and communication we construct an *intersubjective* world out of our individual, subjective worlds. By showing that objectivity is simply not possible, that subjectivity is not always a problem, and that intersubjectivity addresses those instances where the subjectivity of knowledge does become a problem, Dewey presents us with a position that helps us to overcome the stalemate between objectivism and subjectivism. He also hints at a way in which we can overcome the Cartesian Anxiety by showing that we do not have to give up the world when we want to acknowledge that knowledge is always plural, changing and open, and that knowing, most importantly, is always a thoroughly *human* endeavour.

Discussion: pedagogy, knowledge, curriculum, and co-ordination

What then has Dewey to contribute to the discussion about knowledge and the curriculum? One thing that is attractive about Dewey's views is that they can make sense of many of the intuitions we hold about knowledge and the world. Rather than creating an opposition between what philosophy tells us and what we seem to be experiencing in our everyday lives, Dewey's ideas are able to capture many of these experiences. Dewey is able to account for the possibility of making a distinction between truth and falsehood; he helps us to see that realism is a reasonable assumption; he can account for the openness of interpretation while at the same time acknowledging that not anything goes; and his transactional approach can also make sense of the advances in technology (see also Hickman, 1990). Perhaps Dewey even opens up some possibilities for the idea that we can sometimes indeed speak truth to power.

What is different and distinctive about Dewey's approach is that he does not start from the assumption of dualism of mind and world, but urges us to start from somewhere else and, in doing so, to question and overcome the founding assumptions of modern philosophy rather than positioning ourselves within this framework. In this regard, Dewey does indeed manage to go *beyond* objectivism and relativism, to use the title of Bernstein's (1983) book – and the word 'beyond' is of course of tremendous significance here.

This, as I have tried to make clear, has a number of important implications for the discussion about knowledge, experience, and reality. It means the end of the idea of knowledge as a picture of reality and instead puts forward the suggestion that our knowledge is always about *relationships* between actions and consequences. While this does mean that knowledge is a construction, it is not a construction happening somewhere in our head, but a construction 'in transaction', which means that knowledge is both constructed *and* real. From this angle, the question of truth ceases to be a spatial matter – that is of the relationship between statements about the world and the world itself – and instead becomes thoroughly temporal – that is, concerned with the relationship between actions and their consequences. Knowledge thus moves from the domain of certainty, the domain of 'what is', to the domain of *possibility*, the domain of 'what might be the case'.

These observations are, however, still relatively abstract. So what kind of difference would these ideas make if we take a (slightly) more concrete issue concerning knowledge and the curriculum. Let us briefly look at a rather 'strong' example, that of the question of Creationism versus Darwinism.[7] The quick way of addressing this issue is to say that from a Deweyan perspective both Creationism and Darwinism move from the sphere of *certainty* to the sphere of *possibility*, and the most important point to make here is that they express *different* possibilities which have meaning in relation to different human endeavours and different human concerns. The question which one is true is, from that angle, no longer a relevant question to ask, at least not in the abstract or representational sense of truth. The question rather is what Creationism and Darwinism allow us to do in relation to specific human endeavours, and it is only within the confines of that particular question that the issue of truth may be meaningful – not, however, to compare Creationism and Darwinism against some abstract external standard like 'the world out there', but to raise questions about what can be asserted with warrant in relation to always specific endeavours. To say that Creationism and Darwinism have to be understood in terms of possibility rather than certainty and that these questions always have to be raised in relation to specific matters of concern, is not to say that everything is relative, that there is only opinion and taste, and that judgement is no longer possible. The point rather is that our judgements need to be thoroughly pragmatised, that is, they always need to be made in relation to *specific* matters of concern and in relation to *specific* aims and ends. After all, the most important question to ask from the point of view of pragmatism is not 'What is true?' but 'What is the problem?'

While this opens up new, and in my opinion, exciting opportunities for engaging with questions of knowledge and the curriculum, there is one more technical point that I briefly wish to mention (for more on this see Biesta, 2009b, 2011). The point is that in the first section of this paper I have argued that neither the sociology of knowledge nor the philosophy of knowledge can act as a neutral arbiter in discussions about knowledge and the curriculum. It now may seem that by introducing Dewey into the discussion I am trying to do the very thing that I argued earlier to be impossible, that is, presenting Dewey's ideas as a kind of 'über-truth' or meta-narrative that can settle all our problems once and for all. That is not what I am trying to do here – although I am aware that this problem can be a real one (see Biesta, 2009b). One way to address this issue is to make sure that we approach Dewey's own work pragmatically, which means that we should not see it as a new truth about the universe and everything in it, but rather as an attempt to address a very specific problem (see also Biesta, 2010c).

The problem Dewey ultimately sought to address had to do with the impact of modern science on what he referred to as the world of 'common sense' (see Dewey, 1939). While Dewey was happy to acknowledge the advances of modern science and technology, he was concerned about the way in which the scientific worldview was colonising alternative understandings and, more specifically, was also colonising alternative rationalities. Dewey was concerned, in other words, about the way in which the worldview of modern science had become hegemonic, not only in terms of what we hold to be true but also in terms of what we hold to be rational. Dewey's project, so we might say, was therefore one that aimed to overcome the hegemony of modern science, not in an attempt to deny its achievements, but to reject the idea that it is only science that provides us with access to reality as it really is and that it therefore is only science that can provide us with a standard of what is reasonable or rational (see Biesta & Burbules, 2003).

For Dewey, the nub of the problem had to do with the fact that modern science had been interpreted through philosophical categories that predated modern science – such as the idea of truth as having to do with what is permanent and fixed and of knowledge as having to do with an unchanging reality 'out there'. Dewey's project, in a sense, was to explore what would happen if, rather than to interpret modern science through pre-scientific philosophical categories, we would interpret science and its claims to knowledge in its own terms. And the outcome of that exercise, as we have seen, is precisely that science can no longer claim to be the possessor of ultimate truth and ultimate rationality. While, at a superficial level, Dewey's work might seem to be singing the praises of modern science, it actually amounts to one of the most fundamental and strategically effective criticisms of the impact of the scientific worldview on modern society. While there is, of course, much more to say about this, it is important to bear this in mind in order not to assume that Dewey is just trying to present us with another 'philosophy to end all philosophies'.

What then, does all this mean for the discussion with which I started this paper, that is, the question of pedagogy, the idea of co-ordination, and the question what knowledge and the curriculum have to do in relation to this? Let me make two points here. The first is that if we follow Dewey we have to shift our understanding of knowledge and the curriculum from the domain of certainty to the domain of the possible. This has to do be done in a very careful and very precise way, one that proceeds pragmatically – that is, always in relation to matters of human concern – and not relativistically – which would be by suggesting that anything goes, which it obviously does not. The second point concerns the idea of co-ordination. What I have tried to make clear in my reconstruction of Dewey's theory of knowing is that co-ordination is the absolutely central and fundamental process through which we turn our subjective worlds into an intersubjective world (which in itself will always be a plural, overlapping, and conflictual world) – a world, in Dewey's language, communicated, and shared. Schools are, of course, not the only place where such co-ordination happens or should happen, but they are also definitely not insignificant. That is why the idea of co-ordination is important, not only in terms of process – that is, pedagogy – but precisely also in terms of curricular content and educational achievement, and it is precisely there that matters of pedagogy and matters of curriculum connect.

Notes

1. Within the confines of this paper, I wish to focus on what pragmatism and more specifically John Dewey's pragmatism may have to offer for the discussion about knowledge and the curriculum. A more detailed discussion of Young's argument and the differences between the form of social realist philosophy he favours and the transactional realism of Dewey is beyond the scope of this paper. Also, my main aim is to rectify common perceptions about Dewey's pragmatism the paper is not meant to suggest that I agree with or support Dewey's views.
2. The actual formulation in the *Plan of Organization of the University Primary School* is: "The ultimate problem of all education is to co ordinate the psychological and the social factors" (Dewey, 1895, p. 224).
3. This is not to suggest that he was the first to do so; see for example Young (1971).
4. For this I refer the reader to Biesta and Burbules (2003) and Biesta (2009a, 2009b, 2010b).
5. The latter view was the one put forward by logical positivism and, although philosophically discredited, still lives on in the idea that knowledge acquisition is an inductive process

starting from the collection of 'basic facts' and working 'upwards' towards general statements (see Ayer, 1959; Achinstein & Barker, 1969).
6. Dewey's approach is sometimes characterised as instrumentalism, also by Dewey himself. Whereas instrumentalism is generally taken as the view that *theories* are instruments or tools, Dewey's instrumentalism is about the instrumental character of objects of knowledge.
7. Journell (2013) discusses the same issue in a recent article in this journal, but takes a social justice and mutual learning perspective. The point I am making here with Dewey follows an epistemological argument, albeit that it is a pragmatist approach to epistemology that is being pursued here, not one that operates on the assumption of the dualism of mind and world — which is an important point, as Dewey was actually highly suspicious of the whole 'epistemological industry' that had emerged on the basis of this assumption.

References

Achinstein, P., & Barker, S. F. (1969). *The legacy of logical positivism: Studies in the philosophy of science*. Baltimore, MD: Johns Hopkins Press.
Apple, M. (1991). *Ideology and curriculum*. New York, NY: Routledge.
Apple, M. W. (1996). *Cultural politics and education*. New York, NY: Teachers College Press.
Ayer, A. J. (1959). *Logical positivism*. Glencoe, IL: Free Press.
Balarin, M. (2008). Post-structuralism, realism and the question of knowledge in educational sociology. *Policy Futures in Education, 6*(4), 507–519.
Bernstein, B. (1971). *Class, code and control. Volume 1: Theoretical studies towards a sociology of language*. London: Routledge & Kegan Paul.
Bernstein, R. J. (1983). *Beyond objectivism and relativism: Science, hermeneutics, and praxis*. Philadelphia, PA: University of Pennsylvania Press.
Biesta, G. J. J. (2006). '"Of all affairs, communication is the most wonderful." Education as communicative praxis.' In D. T. Hansen (Ed.), *John Dewey and our educational prospect: A critical engagement with Dewey's democracy and education* (pp. 23–37). Albany, NY: SUNY Press.
Biesta, G. J. J. (2007). Why 'what works' won't work: Evidence-based practice and the democratic deficit of educational research. *Educational Theory, 57*(1), 1–22.
Biesta, G. J. J. (2009a). Pragmatism's contribution to understanding learning-in-context. In R. Edwards, G. J. J. Biesta, & M. Thorpe (Eds.), *Rethinking contexts for teaching and learning: Communities, activities and networks* (pp. 61–73). London: Routledge.
Biesta, G. J. J. (2009b). How to use pragmatism pragmatically: Suggestions for the 21st century. In A. G. Rud, J. Garrison, & L. Stone (Eds.), *John Dewey at 150: Reflections for a new century* (pp. 30–39). Lafayette, IN: Purdue University Press.
Biesta, G. J. J. (2010a). *Good education in an age of measurement: Ethics, politics, democracy*. Boulder, CO: Paradigm.
Biesta, G. J. J. (2010b). Pragmatism and the philosophical foundations of mixed methods research. In A. Tashakkori & C. Teddlie (Eds.), *Sage handbook of mixed methods in social and behavioral research* (2nd ed., pp. 95–118). Thousand Oaks, CA: Sage.

Biesta, G. J. J. (2010c). "This is my truth, tell me yours." Deconstructive pragmatism as a philosophy for education. *Educational Philosophy and Theory, 42*(7), 710 727.

Biesta, G. J. J. (2011). Welches Wissen ist am meisten wert? Zur Veränderung des öffentlichen Status von Wissenschaft und Wissen im Feld der Erziehung [Which knowledge is of most worth? On the transformation of the public status of research and knowledge in the field of education]. In: A. Schäfer & C. Thompson (Eds.), *Wissen* (pp. 77 97). Paderborn: Schöningh Verlag.

Biesta, G. J. J. (2013a). Interrupting the politics of learning. *Power and Education, 5*(1), 4 15.

Biesta, G. J. J. (2013b). Responsive or responsible? Education for the global networked society. *Policy Futures in Education, 11*(6), 734 745.

Biesta, G. J. J. & Burbules, N. (2003). *Pragmatism and educational research*. Lanham, MD: Rowman and Littlefield.

Bloor, D. (1983). *Wittgenstein: A social theory of meaning.* London: Macmillan.

Böhme, G., Van den Daele, W., Hohlfeld, R., Krohn, W., & Schäfer, W. (1983). *Finalization in science: The social orientation of scientific progress*. Dordrecht: Reidel.

Dancy, J. (1985). *An introduction of contemporary epistemology*. Oxford: Basil Blackwell.

Dewey, J. (1895). Plan of organization of the university primary school. In J. A. Boydston (Ed.), *The early works (1882 1898), volume 5* (pp. 96 109). Carbondale and Edwardsville: Southern Illinois University Press.

Dewey, J. (1896). The reflex arc concept in psychology. In J. A. Boydston (Ed.), *The early works (1882 1898), volume 5* (pp. 224 243). Carbondale and Edwardsville: Southern Illinois University Press.

Dewey, J. (1905). The postulate of immediate empricism. In J. A. Boydston (Ed.), *The middle works (1899 1924), volume 3* (pp. 158 167). Carbondale and Edwardsville: Southern Illinois University Press.

Dewey, J. (1906). The experimental theory of knowledge. In J. A. Boydston (Ed.), *The middle works (1899 1924), volume 3* (pp. 107 127). Carbondale and Edwardsville: Southern Illinois University Press.

Dewey, J. (1907). The control of ideas by facts. In J. A. Boydston (Ed.), *The middle works (1899 1924), volume 4* (pp. 78 90). Carbondale and Edwardsville: Southern Illinois University Press.

Dewey, J. (1911). Epistemology. In J. A. Boydston (Ed.), *The middle works (1899 1924), volume 6* (pp. 440 442). Carbondale and Edwardsville: Southern Illinois University Press.

Dewey, J. (1916). Introduction to essays in experimental logic. In J. A. Boydston (Ed.), *The middle works (1899 1924), volume 10* (pp. 320 369). Carbondale and Edwardsville: Southern Illinois University Press.

Dewey, J. (1920). Reconstruction in philosophy. In J. A. Boydston (Ed.), *The middle works (1899 1924), volume 12* (pp. 77 201). Carbondale and Edwardsville: Southern Illinois University Press.

Dewey, J. (1922). Human nature and conduct. In J. A. Boydston (Ed.), *The middle works (1899 1924), volume 14.* Carbondale and Edwardsville: Southern Illinois University Press.

Dewey, J. (1925). Experience and nature. In J. A. Boydston (Ed.), *The Later Works (1925 1953), volume 1.* Carbondale and Edwardsville: Southern Illinois University Press.

Dewey, J. (1929). The quest for certainty. In J. A. Boydston (Ed.), *The later works (1925 1953), volume 4.* Carbondale and Edwardsville: Southern Illinois University Press.

Dewey, J. (1933). How we think: A restatement of the relation of reflective thinking to the educative process. In J. A. Boydston (Ed.), *The later works (1925 1953), volume 8* (pp. 105 352). Carbondale and Edwardsville: Southern Illinois University Press.

Dewey, J. (1939). Experience, knowledge and value: A rejoinder. In J. A. Boydston (Ed.), *The later works (1925 1953), volume 14* (pp. 3 90). Carbondale and Edwardsville: Southern Illinois University Press.

Dewey, J., & Bentley, A. F. (1949). *Knowing and the known*. Boston, MA: Beacon Press.

Foucault, M. (1984). What is enlightenment? In P. Rabinow (Ed.), *The foucault reader* (pp. 32 50). New York, NY: Pantheon Books.

Gellner, E. (1992). *Postmodernism, reason and religion*. London: Routledge.

Hickman, L. (1990). *John Dewey's pragmatic technology*. Bloomington: Indiana University Press.

Horkheimer, M. (1947). *Eclipse of reason*. New York, NY: Oxford University Press.

Journell, W. (2013). Learning from each other: What social studies can learn from the controversy surrounding the teaching of evolution in science. *The Curriculum Journal, 24*(4), 494 510.

Kliebard, H. M. (1987). *The struggle for the American curriculum, 1893 1958*. New York, NY: Routledge & Kegan Paul.

Nozick, R. (1981). *Philosophical explanations*. Oxford: Oxford University Press.

Sleeper, R. W. (1986). *The necessity of pragmatism: John Dewey's conception of philosophy*. New Haven, CT: Yale University Press.

Spencer, W. (1909). *Education: Intellectual, moral, and physical*. New York, NY: Appleton.

Young, M. (Ed.). (1971). *Knowledge and control*. London: Collier Macmillan.

Young, M. (2008). *Bringing knowledge back in: From social constructivism to social realism in the sociology of education*. London: Routledge.

Young, M., & Muller, J. (2007). Truth and truthfulness in the sociology of educational knowledge. *Theory and Research in Education, 5*, 173 201.

Young, M., & Muller, J. (2008). The cosmic community: A response to Maria Balarin's 'Post-structuralism, realism and the question of knowledge in educational sociology. *Policy Futures in Education, 6*(4), 519 523.

Downgraded curriculum? An analysis of knowledge in new curricula in Scotland and New Zealand

Mark Priestley[a] and Claire Sinnema[b]

[a]School of Education, University of Stirling, Stirling, UK; [b]School of Learning, Development and Professional Practice, The University of Auckland, Auckland, New Zealand

> The development, since 2000, of new national curricula across the Anglophone world signals a number of policy trends, including: a move from the explicit specification of content towards a more generic, skill-based approach; a greater emphasis on the centrality of the learner; and [ostensibly] greater autonomy for teachers in developing the curriculum in school. These policy shifts have attracted some criticism, especially from social realist writers, who claim that the new curricula downgrade knowledge. This paper offers a contribution to this debate; an empirically based analysis of two new curricula, New Zealand's Curriculum Framework and Scotland's Curriculum for Excellence. We conclude that, while these curricula continue to accord considerable importance to knowledge in their statements of policy intent, the social realist critique is at least partially justified, since both curricula are characterised by a lack of coherence and mixed messages about the place of knowledge.

> New Zealand's school curriculum has been hollowed out of knowledge as academic learning is increasingly abandoned for a misguided focus on skills and the process of learning. (New Zealand Herald, 2013)

Introduction

Since the turn of the millennium, Anglophone education systems have witnessed a curricular turn (for an overview of trends and commonalities, see Sinnema & Aitken, 2013; see also Wheelahan, 2010; Young, 2009). This 'new curriculum' (Biesta & Priestley, 2013) is associated with moves prompted by globalisation to position education systems more widely, and curriculum in particular, as drivers of economic development and national competitiveness (Yates & Young, 2010). While the 'new curriculum' varies in form from country to country, researchers have identified a number of common features. It is claimed that these include: a shift from the prescriptive specification of knowledge content evident in many earlier national curricula to what Young (2008) has termed genericism[1]; a new focus on the centrality of the learner, accompanied by the development of active forms of pedagogy and a view of teachers as facilitators of learning (Sinnema & Aitken, 2013); the articulation of curriculum as assessable outcomes, modular courses and ladders of qualifications (Young, 2008), accompanied by increasingly pervasive regimes of accountability and cultures of performativity (Priestley, Robinson, & Biesta, 2012).

The 'new curriculum' has attracted its share of controversy and criticism, as illustrated by the quotation at the head of this paper, taken from a New Zealand daily newspaper.[2] It is this critique of a claimed 'downgrading' of knowledge (Yates & Collins, 2010) in the 'new curriculum' that provides the focus for this paper. We first provide a brief overview and analysis of the critique provided by social realists such as Michael Young. Social realism has offered a powerful critique of modern trends in curriculum development – arguably the most significant challenge to what they refer to as technical-instrumentalist curricula (Moore & Young, 2001) – and is thus fundamental to any treatment of the issue of knowledge and the 'new curriculum', whether one agrees or not with their arguments. In this paper, we offer an empirical contribution to these recent debates about curriculum and knowledge, examining the extent to which the above claims about the downgrading of knowledge are justified. In doing so, we draw upon two case studies, Scotland's *Curriculum for Excellence* and the *New Zealand Curriculum*, both of which exhibit many of the common features outlined above.

Knowledge and the 'new curriculum'

Social realist writers (for example, Rata, 2012b; Wheelahan, 2010; Young, 2007) have highlighted a worldwide trend for new curricular models to downgrade knowledge. Their critique is reflected to some extent in anxieties expressed more widely about the curricular turn towards technical-instrumentalism (for example, Biesta, 2011; Ecclestone, 2013; Priestley, 2011; Watson, 2010; Yates & Collins, 2010).

This curricular turn has at least two dimensions. First, critics point to an overt shift from the specification of disciplinary knowledge to an emphasis on the development of generic skills, often with an instrumental focus on citizenship and/or the workplace. Within our two case studies, the specification of key capacities or competencies to be achieved by education might be seen as evidence of this shift: Scotland's *Curriculum for Excellence* aims to develop students as successful learners, confident individuals, effective contributors and responsible citizens (Scottish

Executive, 2004a); in similar fashion, the *New Zealand Curriculum* specifies five key competencies – thinking, using language, symbols and texts, managing self, relating to others, participating and contributing (New Zealand Ministry of Education, 2007). This new focus on 'setting out not what children are expected to know, but how they should be' (Watson, 2010, p. 99) is seen by some to be sinister, with overtones of indoctrination and totalitarianism. It has also been alleged by critics to oversimplify and dichotomise the complex relationship between knowledge and skills, obscuring the relationship between different forms of knowledge. For example, Young (2009) has questioned whether such generic skills can indeed be developed free of contextual knowledge and 'free of the domains in which they are realised' (p. 4).

The turn towards competencies and capabilities in many of the most recent revisions to national curricula gives rise to the question of temporality in the emergence and circulation the 'new curriculum'. That question deserves detailed attention that is beyond the scope of this paper. It is clear, though, that there is 'cross-national attraction associated with policy borrowing', described by Phillips and Ochs (2003) across global curriculum policy, for example, in the case of lifelong learning. That concept has become, due to policy diffusion, widely adopted in education policy, according to Jakobi (2012). The wide adoption, she suggests, is due to the success of international organisations in disseminating educational policy ideas which lead to common goals across nations. A second example lies in the specification of competencies and capabilities in national curricula; the Organisation for Economic Development 'DeSeCo' project (Definition and Selection of Competencies) is widely cited as influencing the inclusion of such competencies in curriculum.

A second key feature of the social realist critique lies in the distinction between everyday and disciplinary knowledge, and the increasing emphasis on interdisciplinary approaches to organising the curriculum has thus attracted their criticism. For instance, Young and Muller (2010) have claimed that a weakening of traditional subject boundaries is problematic. They see an erosion of the distinction between academic knowledge and everyday knowledge, a weakening of the relations between the knowledge in academic disciplines and what is taught in schools, and an attendant danger that, in the lack of specification of content, less experienced teachers will 'fall behind without knowing it, or miss out conceptual steps that may be vital later on' (p. 23). They claim that denying young people access to the 'powerful knowledge' enshrined in disciplines is detrimental to their life chances, a theme echoed by Rata (2012a, 2012b), who warns of the social exclusion inherent in the 'new curriculum'. Such views are rooted in an 'assumption [...] that *the acquisition of knowledge* is the key purpose that distinguishes education, whether general, further, vocational or higher, from all other activities' (Young, 2007, p. 81, emphasis in original).

As stated above, the issue of knowledge in the curriculum has been a cause for concern amongst educationalists beyond social realism. However, whether Wheelahan's (2010) 'crisis of curriculum' is a reality is more open to debate. There are a number of caveats to offer here. First, one might question whether the distinction between everyday knowledge and disciplinary knowledge is as clear-cut as might be suggested by some of the social realist literature or indeed whether skills and knowledge are as neatly separable as suggested. For example, Gill and Thomson (2012) suggest that this is a false dichotomy, and that high-level knowledge is really the skill of being able to differentiate between concepts. Linked to these questions is the issue of whether it is appropriate for the school curriculum to focus entirely on disciplinary knowledge; it is fair to say that the powerful arguments of the social realists are countered by equally powerful discourses that suggest that it is the business of schools to shape the individual, develop attributes and dispositions and teach everyday knowledge that has practical utility for everyday life (for example, see Gardner, 1991; Kelly, 1999; White, 2011). Such authors have offered progressive views of curriculum, whereby content is selected to address educational purposes, for example the development of the potential for active citizenship, rather than being included in the curriculum because it reflects disciplinary knowledge. This is not to suggest that such approaches negate the place of knowledge in curriculum or even the selection and organisation of content through traditionally recognised subjects. For example, Dewey (1907) explicitly rejected what he saw as the false dichotomy of knowledge and process, emphasising the importance of the 'accumulated wisdom of the world'.

Second, even if we accept the premise that school knowledge should be drawn from disciplines, this is not the same as saying that it should be framed around traditional subjects as is sometimes advocated by social realists. As Whitty (2010) points out, 'knowledge is not the same as school subjects and school subjects are not the same thing as academic disciplines' (p. 34). It is perfectly possible to conceive alternative rigorous approaches to teaching disciplinary knowledge that are interdisciplinary in nature, rather than being framed as traditional subjects (for example, see Beane, 1997). The social realist literature tends to advocate traditionalist approaches to defining school subjects, but is less clear in delineating subjects from disciplines than it is in illustrating how knowledge is socially formed into disciplines. In the latter case, a convincing case is made for the intellectual legitimation of knowledge over time within the institutional structures of academic disciplines. Here, drawing upon the work of Bernstein (1990), both the social origins and academic legitimacy of disciplinary knowledge are clearly demonstrated. However, the case is less clearly made for justifying school subjects, social constructs like disciplines, but arguably lacking their high level of intellectual legitimacy (see Goodson & Marsh, 1996)

A third issue for debate is hinted at in Young's (2007) distinction between routinised and reflexive engagement with knowledge. Young, drawing upon Davydov, points out that 'much of schooling [consists] of the routinized [sic] acquisition of scientific concepts' (p. 53). Thus it is not clear, even where school knowledge is disciplinary in origin in line with social realist arguments, that it necessarily constitutes the sort of powerful knowledge advocated by Young. It is worth noting here that 'new curricula' around the globe tend to advocate active and constructivist forms of pedagogy that are said to encourage the development of deep understanding of concepts (presumably reflexive acquisition of knowledge), but that many social realists reject these approaches as synonymous with relativist, constructionist notions of knowledge (for example, Rata, 2012b).

While we briefly note the above issues as interesting facets of the debate on knowledge in the curriculum, they are nevertheless peripheral to this paper. Our interest here has a more practical focus, concerning the degree to which social realist claims about the downgrading of knowledge in the 'new curriculum' are empirically sustainable. For the purposes of this paper we examine two examples of the 'new curriculum, Scotland's Curriculum for Excellence (CfE) and the New Zealand Curriculum. There are two levels of analysis undertaken in the paper:

- *At the high level of curriculum statements, or in terms of policy intention*. The key question here is whether these curricula sufficiently emphasise the importance of knowledge, or whether the social realists are justified in making the claims that they downgrade knowledge.
- *At the operational level of the working documents*. Our concern here is to identify whether the working documents of the curricula provide adequate guidance for practitioners as they develop the curriculum *in situ*. There are two main approaches to facilitate the specification of content at this level: the first is the specification of 'important content', that is input regulation of the curriculum (Nieveen & Kuiper, 2012); the second relates to the existence or otherwise of clear processes for content specification, to guide practitioners as they engage in school-based curriculum development.

The case study contexts

Before undertaking our analysis, we first provide a brief overview of the background and key features of each curriculum. Space precludes a detailed description or analysis.

The curriculum for excellence case

CfE was launched in 2004, when the Scottish Executive published a paper titled *A Curriculum for Excellence: The Curriculum Review Group*

(Scottish Executive, 2004a). The central feature of CfE is the specification of four key capacities, along with accompanying descriptor statements, which are to be promoted through a child's education: successful learners; confident individuals; responsible citizens; effective contributors (p. 12).

The 2004 discussion paper did not offer an extended justification for its terminology or structure, and should be regarded as a macro-level framework, designed to form the basis of subsequent policy development. It was accompanied by the Ministerial Response (Scottish Executive, 2004b), which set out future directions for the new curriculum in a more concrete manner than did the review document, laying out, for example, that the new curriculum would be articulated as 'clear statements of the outcomes which each young person should aspire to achieve' (p. 4) and hinting that subjects would continue to be the basis of the curriculum. In 2006, the publication of *A Curriculum for Excellence: Progress and Proposals* (Scottish Executive, 2006) added more detail, emphasising the importance of engagement by teachers, the centrality of learning and teaching and the unification of the curriculum from 3 to 18. This document outlined a series of six sequential levels, establishing the principle that 'expectations will be described in terms of experiences as well as broad significant outcomes' and that these would be 'designed to reflect the Four Capacities' (p. 12). Significantly, it was proposed at this stage that the curriculum would be structured around domains of knowledge, as was the case for previous Scottish curricula.[3]

Further guidance has emerged since 2006. This includes the *Building the Curriculum* series, which, for example, has provided additional guidance on the eight curricular categories outlined above, the early years curriculum and assessment, and experiences and outcomes (Es & Os) in each of eight curricular areas (Education Scotland, 2013). These follow a formulaic structure, seeking to combine within simple statements, set out in hierarchical levels, both the expected outcomes of learning and the experiences through which the outcomes might be achieved. The following examples from Science give a flavour of these:

> By contributing to experiments and investigations, I can develop my understanding of models of matter and can apply this to changes of state and the energy involved as they occur in nature. [SCN 2-05a]
>
> Through research on how animals communicate, I can explain how sound vibrations are carried by waves through air, water and other media. [SCN 2-11a]
>
> (Education Scotland, 2013)

The New Zealand Curriculum case

The New Zealand Curriculum (NZC) was launched in 2007 following a curriculum stocktake (Le Métais, 2002; Australian Council of

Educational Research, 2002) and a lengthy and inclusive curriculum development process between 2004 and 2007. That process involved more than 15,000 students, teachers, principals, advisers and academics in the development, trialling and response to a draft curriculum in 2006 and the subsequent revisions in the 2007 final version.

Key shifts in the New Zealand Ministry of Education (2007) from previous curricula were the inclusion of all learning areas in a single policy document, the specification of key competencies (rather than essential skills) – thinking, using language, symbols and texts, managing self, relating to others, participating and contributing, a section on effective pedagogy, and the repositioning of specific achievement objectives as guidelines (leaving single-page learning area statements as the compulsory aspect). The NZC is also characterised by an emphasis on school-level curriculum autonomy and flexibility – the document is intentionally broad, with a section on school-based curriculum design and review that places the onus for development of school-level curriculum firmly on practitioners. In this way, the policy achieves the goal set out in the development process of reducing, refining and clarifying the curriculum – curriculum intentions are set out in broad terms and it signals that responsibility for specifics rests with schools.

Like CfE, the NZC continued the tradition of using domains of knowledge as a curriculum organiser – while guidance suggested those domains not be required as the structure for delivery of the curriculum, learning areas persisted as a means of organising achievement objectives. The following examples from science, social studies and mathematics illustrate their format:

> Students will recognise that there are life processes common to all living things and that these occur in different ways. (Science, Level 3, Living World)
>
> Students will gain knowledge, skills and experience to: Understand how groups make and implement rules and laws. (Social Sciences, Level 3)
>
> In a range of meaningful contexts, students will be engaged in thinking mathematically and statistically. They will solve problems and model situations that require them to: Use a range of additive and simple multiplicative strategies with whole numbers, fractions, decimals, and percentages. (Mathematics and Statistics, Level 3, Number)

A national evaluation of the implementation of the NZC (Sinnema, 2011) revealed that educators in both primary and secondary schools held the curriculum in high regard. They typically viewed it positively, considered it to be an improvement on the previous curriculum, and were committed to implementing it. That commitment was somewhat challenged by policies released soon after the NZC, outlining national standards for reading, writing and mathematics. While described by the Ministry of

Education as standards to support the curriculum itself, many educators believed that the stipulation of national standards and the subsequent necessity to focus on traditional curriculum outcomes compromised the freedom and autonomy needed to give effect to a curriculum that was broad, forward-looking and responded to local needs and desires.

Methodology

In conducting our analysis, we used a case study approach, employing document analysis to examine curriculum policy texts from the two contexts. The purpose of looking to policies from both countries was not specifically to compare the contexts of these two curricula, but rather to enable broader consideration of the ways in which they position knowledge. The document analysis approach (Rapley & Jenkings, 2010) dealt with actual textual content – we examined the frequency, nature and type of mentions of knowledge using quantitative content analysis (Weber, 1990). It also dealt with extra-textual content of the documents, as we analysed the contextual and design features of the curriculum policy texts (organisation and structure) that provide messages about the status of knowledge, using qualitative content analysis (Pickering, 2004).

Research questions

Within the two levels of analysis specified above, we posed the following questions relating to the overarching question about whether these curricula downgrade knowledge:

(1) How is knowledge positioned in national curricula statements of intent?
(2) How is knowledge positioned in operational guidance aspects of national curricula?
(3) How consistent are the messages about the positioning of knowledge in curricular policy?
(4) Do these curricula downgrade knowledge?

Sampling and analysis

There are multiple documents that outline CfE,[4] in contrast with just one English-medium document in New Zealand.[5] Therefore, when analysing the two sets of documents, we needed to give careful consideration to identifying sections of text that are directly comparable in their attention function as providing statements of intent (both overall and for curriculum/learning areas) and operational guidance. The selection of these documents and sections of them was also based on their status as key policy documents, recognised as such by practitioners. Furthermore, they were considered likely sites of signals about the position of knowledge in the curriculum, since they set out both curriculum intentions and operational guidance.

Statements of intent included in the analysis from the NZC were drawn from the section typically referred to in New Zealand as 'the front end', which outlines overall curriculum purpose (pages 1–15) and the series of pages in the middle of the document that outline statements of purpose for each of the eight learning areas (pages 16–33). Equivalent material from CfE was drawn from 'Building the Curriculum 3: A Framework for Learning and Teaching' and also the statements about 'Principles and Practice' relating to each curriculum area in the 'CfE Experiences and Outcomes' document.

The CfE 3 sections indicated above were selected since they were comparable to the NZC statements of intent. They outlined overall curriculum purpose and structure in relation to the Scottish curriculum and, while duplicating ideas presented in the 2004 review document, these sections provided an overall framework most similar in scope and level of detail to that of the NZC. The sections introducing each curriculum area in the 'CfE Experiences and Outcomes document' (preceding the pages with tables of outcomes) were similar in nature to the 'one-pagers' about each learning area in the NZC.

Operational guidance included in the analysis from the NZC was situated in the achievement objectives set out for each of the learning areas for the eight achievement levels of the curriculum. The CfE-equivalent material is found in the introductory statements and statements of experiences and outcomes in the 'CfE Experiences and Outcomes' document.

These sections of operational guidance from the two curricula were selected since they were similar in scope and detail. The levelled statements of specific desired outcomes in the NZC are organised around learning areas, just as the CfE statements of specific experiences and outcomes are organised around curriculum areas at particular levels.

To address the first research question, we subjected the main macro-level documents to a keyword search for mentions of the terms 'knowledge', 'knowledges' and 'know'. Entire sentences in which those terms were used were added to a database for analysis. Mentions relating specifically to 'prior knowledge' were excluded, since these typically referred to desired pedagogical approaches (linking to prior knowledge) rather than to desired outcomes. A deductive coding framework was developed to examine how knowledge is positioned in each curriculum, for example the extent to which knowledge is treated as an end (having intrinsic value), or as a means (having instrumental value), and the extent to which it is treated as an exclusive aim or not. The framework is outlined in Appendix A.

Data were analysed using SPSS. This allowed calculation of frequency counts of total references to knowledge in each of the curricula along with references categorised, for example, as having intrinsic or instrumental value. Using cross tabs we were able to compare whether the references outlined above were in statements of intent or in statements of operational guidance. To establish inter-rater reliability in the coding outlined above, a random sample of just over 10% of the total knowledge statements (n 60) were coded by a second coder, who disagreed with the original coder on only 2 of the 120 coding decisions for those statements, indicating inter-rater reliability in excess of 98%.

To address the second research question, we looked specifically at the messages relating to knowledge that aimed more explicitly at framing practice. Analysis of these documents focused on two main aspects: (1) the positioning of references to knowledge in relation to disciplines, domains of knowledge and/or subjects and (2) the positioning of references to knowledge relative to other curricular elements, such as skills, competencies and capabilities.

Throughout the analysis of both macro-level intentions and specific curricular guidance, we were concerned to track the consistency of messages about knowledge as well as their overall clarity and specificity, and to ultimately address the question of whether these curricula downgrade knowledge.

Findings

Curricular emphases on knowledge in policy intentions and operational guidance

We first examined how these curricula make general references to knowledge. As expected, there were multiple references to knowledge in both the NZC (n 128) and the CfE (n 270) documents analysed. While it did not make sense to directly compare the above frequency counts, since the size of the documents varied, it is valid to compare the proportions of such references since this indicates the priority given within the curricula to knowledge. It is therefore significant that more than 17% of the mentions of knowledge in the NZC sources were in sections outlining curricular intent. This compares with less than 5% within CfE. In both policies, the premise that knowledge matters is apparent through the positioning of statement promoting knowledge in prominent high-level sections of the documents. For example, the CfE policy framework states clearly that:

> All children and young people in Scotland have an entitlement to a curriculum which will support them in developing their values and beliefs and enable them to: develop knowledge and understanding of society, the world and Scotland's place in it. (CfE, Building the Curriculum 3, p. 14)

Similarly, in the NZC foreword (New Zealand Ministry of Education, 2007), knowledge is the first in a list of purposes: 'a framework designed to ensure that all young New Zealanders are equipped with the knowledge, competencies, and values they will need to be successful citizens in the twenty-first century' (p. 4). It also features in statements about the vision set out for young people, who 'will continue to develop the values, knowledge, and competencies that will enable them to live full and satisfying lives' (p. 8). Such statements indicate strongly that the policy intent in both curricula is to emphasise the importance of knowledge in developing the person.

However, in CfE, a greater proportion (31%) of the knowledge references were positioned in the sections about particular curriculum areas than was the case in the NZC (23%). The tendency in the Scottish context for knowledge mentions to be prevalent in curriculum area intention statements perhaps signals a stronger connection between knowledge and the curriculum areas with their disciplinary underpinnings. (However, as we noted previously, the subject domains in CfE were inherited from previous curricula, so this in no way implies that there has been a systematic attempt to redefine curricular content, only that there is perhaps a taken-for-granted assumption that knowledge is important.)

In both contexts, more than 60% of the mentions of knowledge were in the section that outlined specific outcomes (as opposed to more general documentation that related to subject areas): achievement objectives as outlined for each learning area in the case of the NZC, and experiences and outcomes for each curriculum area in the case of CfE:

> Within the modern languages framework young people will demonstrate their progression as they move through levels in terms of increasing awareness of language rules, including knowledge about language. (CfE, Experiences and Outcomes, p. 175)

> As they engage with and develop knowledge and deeper understandings of music, they draw on cultural practices and on histories, theories, structures, technologies and personal experiences. (NZC, The Arts, p. 21)

We will come back in due course to the question of whether these latter references in the outcomes documents are closely linked to disciplinary knowledge, or whether they simply refer to knowledge in a generic way. Table 1 provides detail about the proportions of such references to knowledge in different sections of the curriculum documentation.

Knowledge: end or means?

An interesting question lies in the stated purposes of the acquisition of knowledge. There were some differences between and within the two curricula in relation to mentions of knowledge as an end in its own right,

Table 1. References to knowledge in the New Zealand and Scottish curricula.

	The New Zealand Curriculum (NZC)	Curriculum for Excellence (CfE)	Combined NZC and CfE
Intent: curriculum overall	22 (17.2%)	13 (4.8%)	35 (8.8%)
Intent: curriculum/learning areas	29 (22.7%)	83 (30.7%)	112 (28.1%)
Operational guidance	77 (60.2%)	174 (64.4%)	251 (63.1%)
Total	128 (100%)	270 (100%)	398 (100%)

compared to those framing it as an instrumental means to various purposes. This is illustrated in Table 2.

In both the NZC and CfE there was a greater emphasis on the intrinsic value of knowledge than on the instrumental value of knowledge in sections dealing with overall curriculum and learning area intent. This greater emphasis was most marked in CfE, with more than three times the percentage of mentions of knowledge as end (as opposed to mentions of knowledge as instrumental) in the overall curriculum intent documentation. That pattern, in both NZC and CfE, was reversed in data from the operational guidance sections of the curricula. Here, statements of outcomes and achievement objectives tended to signal slightly greater emphasis on instrumental knowledge, as shown in the following examples:

> Students will: Apply knowledge of the elements of music, structural devices, and technologies through integrating aural, practical, and theoretical skills. (NZC, The Arts, Music Level 4 achievement objective)

> I can use my knowledge and skills of science and mathematics and can apply the basic principles of control technology in solving practical problems. (CfE, Technologies Experiences and Outcomes, Level 4)

Disciplinary or everyday knowledge?

The first part of this paper has dealt primarily with high-level messages about knowledge. A question raised by the social realists, but not yet

Table 2. Knowledge as end, knowledge as means.

	The New Zealand Curriculum		Curriculum for Excellence	
	Knowledge as end	Knowledge as instrumental	Knowledge as end	Knowledge as instrumental
Intent: curriculum overall	12 (9.4%)	10 (7.8%)	10 (3.7%)	3 (1.1%)
Intent: curriculum/learning areas	17 (13.3%)	12 (9.4%)	56 (20.7%)	27 (10%)
Operational guidance	36 (28.1%)	41 (32%)	78 (28.9%)	96 (35.6%)
Total	65 (50.8%)	63 (49.2%)	144 (53.3%)	126 (46.7%)

Note: Percentages indicate the percentage of within country totals.

addressed here, is whether these curricula blur the boundaries between disciplinary versus everyday knowledge. At this level of macro-level messages about knowledge, we make several observations. Many of the references to knowledge are generic, that they do not make explicit the difference between everyday and disciplinary knowledge, and this makes it difficult to differentiate analytically between these categories. Notwithstanding this failure to make explicit this distinction, it is clear that a large number of references (as illustrated by the extracts provided in the text to date) appear to be referring to disciplinary knowledge. The following two examples from the two curricula indicate the importance of disciplinary knowledge in the area of science:

> It involves generating and testing ideas, gathering evidence, including by making observations, carrying out investigations and modelling, and communicating and debating with others – in order to develop scientific knowledge, understanding, and explanations. (NZC, Science, p. 28)

> Children and young people participating in the experiences and outcomes in the sciences will demonstrate a secure knowledge and understanding of the big ideas and concepts of the sciences. (CfE, Building the Curriculum 3, Science, p. 253)

We can therefore conclude here that, at the level of statements of curricular intent at least, the intention is that disciplinary knowledge is accorded a high degree of importance, both in terms of intrinsic and instrumental value.

Policy into practice: the status of knowledge in curricular guidance

We might conclude from the above sections that both curricula, at least at the level of policy intention, place a strong emphasis on knowledge, as evidenced by the frequency with which it is mentioned. As we noted above, many references are generic in nature, failing to specify the nature of such knowledge, for example whether it has its origins in scientific disciplines or not. Nevertheless, one might argue that it is not the job of macro-level policy statements to define the content that is taught in schools – centralised input regulation (Nieveen & Kuiper, 2012) – but instead to develop the conceptual frame within which either teachers might undertake school-based curriculum development. Put differently, the issue is whether 'to put the skills or intended capabilities in the foreground, as the framework, and leave subject-trained teachers to draw on their own expertise to work out how these were to be achieved [... or] to leave subjects in place but to ask schools to work out ways to integrate these to develop the new capabilities' (Yates, Collins, & O'Connor, 2010, p. 316). There are thus legitimate questions about the ways in which CfE and the NZF guidance documentation specify content – in other words whether the policy guidance is more precise than the macro-level statements of intent on the nature of knowledge to be acquired – and whether clear processes are specified to facilitate the development of programmes of content that reflect the importance placed upon knowledge in the high-level policy statements. The following sections of the paper address these issues, drawing empirically on the curricular documentation from both countries.

Curricular design: the place of subjects

In Scotland's *Building the Curriculum 3* (Education Scotland, 2013), a key piece of guidance for schools, there is a specific section on curriculum areas and subjects. This strongly emphasises the essential nature of subjects as a way of structuring knowledge:

> Subjects are an essential feature of the curriculum, particularly in secondary school. They provide an important and familiar structure for knowledge, offering a context for specialists to inspire, stretch and motivate. Throughout a young person's learning there will be increasing specialisation and greater depth, which will lead to subjects increasingly being the principal means of structuring learning and delivering outcomes. (p. 20)

Subject-based curriculum areas also remain a central feature of the NZC. Just as the CfE organises curriculum experiences and outcomes in curriculum areas (expressive arts, health and well-being, languages, mathematics, religious and moral education, science, social studies and technologies), the NZC outlines achievement objectives around eight learning areas (English, the arts, health and physical education, learning languages, mathematics and statistics, science, social sciences and technology). The NZC describes learning associated with the eight areas as 'part of a broad, general education [that] lays a foundation for later specialisation'.

It is quite clear here that students' acquisition of new knowledge is viewed as desirable within both curricula. In both cases, domains of knowledge are specified as the foundation for developing curricular content. In both case, these domains are derived from previous policy. For example, in the Scottish case, one can trace this aspect of policy back to the seminal 1977 Munn report, reaffirming the 'Hirstian subject-based curriculum' (Boyd, 1997, p. 60). This lineage suggests that both curricula thus establish the framework for content that reflects disciplinary knowledge.

However, the situation is less clear-cut than might seem at first glance. Given that matters of skill and competency and the like are also treated as desirable, what messages do the policies give about what matters most? Both curricula are articulated at the sharp end as outcomes, which tend to specify conceptual understandings or concepts or content only in the most general manner. For example:

> Investigate and experience ways in which scientific, technological, and environmental knowledge and resources assist in and influence people's participation in regular physical activity. (NZC, Health and PE Level 5 achievement objective)

> Students will gain knowledge, skills, and experience to understand that people have social, cultural, and economic roles, rights, and responsibilities. (NZC Social Studies Level 2 achievement objective)

> I can use my knowledge of a historical period to interpret the evidence and present an informed view. (CfE, Social Studies Experiences and Outcomes, Level 3)

Minty and Priestley (2012), in their research on the implementation of CfE in one Scottish local authority, noted the potential of the Es & Os to be used by teachers to justify the continuation of existing practices, quoting a teacher who said:

> I can cover all of these assessment parts in one, with one project here, one short project. It's not exactly the way they are saying it, but you are not saying we can't do it this way. And it meets all the criteria. I can tick all the boxes quite confidently. [...] that is one thing that you can see with Curriculum for Excellence: that the rules aren't quite as strict; you can tweak them without feeling too guilty. (p. 20)

Moreover, the focus on outcomes in both curricula neglects to specify processes for specifying knowledge. Our analysis showed clearly that there are no such processes, and we suggest that, along with the generic nature of the outcomes, there is a risk that the nature of knowledge acquired in school will be driven by more immediate concerns – assessment regimes, examinations syllabi, the availability of resources and routinised practices – rather than on consideration of what constitutes powerful knowledge.

Design issues: inconsistencies and lack of coherence and alignment

In our examination of curriculum documentation we noted the prevalence of mixed messages about the status of knowledge. This is especially evident in the extent to which the structure and text of the policies presented inconsistencies in emphasis and a lack of coherence in regard to the position of knowledge. The importance of knowledge is certainly present in statements of curricula intent, but not consistently so – there is a lack of alignment in positioning of knowledge within and across curriculum documents. Our analysis suggests that some texts strongly position knowledge (either exclusively or alongside other aspects, such as skills), whereas others emphasise only other aspects. There were discrepancies across different policy documents regarding the position and status of knowledge. Some curriculum intent statements focus exclusively on knowledge:

> Learning through social studies extends children and young people's horizons and knowledge of time and place, and challenges them to look at the world in new ways. (CfE, Building the Curriculum 1, p. 34)

Others exclude specific mention of knowledge:

> [CfE] should give young people the confidence, attributes and capabilities to make valuable contributions to society. (Scottish Executive, 2004a, p. 11)

Even more (as outlined in Table 3) intent statements include reference to knowledge amongst a set of other desirable aspects.

While these data illustrate that an exclusive focus on knowledge or knowledge and understanding is prevalent in both countries, a closer look at the sets of outcomes is revealing. What strikes us about those sets of outcomes were the inconsistencies within and across policy documents with regard to the aspects they include. As the selection below shows, typically knowledge is included alongside understanding and skills, but various other aspects are inconsistently included. Sometimes capabilities are included (see examples 2, 3 and 8), sometimes they are not (see examples 1, 4, 5, 6, 7 and 9). Sometimes attributes are included (see examples 3, 4, 5 and 8), sometimes they are not (see examples 1, 2, 6, 7 and 9), and similarly for understanding and abilities. There is a sense of the arbitrariness in the construction of these statements about intention, which reduces the coherence of the curriculum for users:

(1) There is more space in the curriculum for work in depth, and to ensure that young people develop the literacy, numeracy and other essential *skills and knowledge* they will need for life and work (Scottish Executive, 2004a, p. 4).
(2) It is designed to convey *knowledge* which is considered to be important and to promote the development of *values, understanding and capabilities* (Scottish Executive, 2004a, p. 9).

Table 3. Knowledge as an exclusive end or part of a set.

	The New Zealand Curriculum (NZC)	Curriculum for Excellence (CfE)	Combined NZC and CfE
Exclusive	44 (67.7%)	75 (52.1%)	119 (56.9%)
Part of a set	21 (32.3%)	69 (47.9%)	90 (43.1%)
Total	65 (100%)	144 (100%)	209 (100%)

Note: Percentages indicate percentage of within country totals.

(3) Taken together, experiences and outcomes across the curriculum areas will sum up national aspirations for every young person: the *knowledge and understanding, skills, capabilities and attributes* we hope they will develop (CfE, Building the Curriculum 1, p. 3).

(4) Learning through health and well-being enables children and young people to: develop the *knowledge and understanding, skills, abilities and attitudes* necessary for their physical, emotional and social well-being now and in their future lives (CfE, Building the Curriculum 1, p. 6).

(5) Approaches to learning and teaching should provide challenge and opportunities for children and young people to develop their *knowledge and understanding, skills and attributes* (CfE, Building the Curriculum 1, p. 10).

(6) In Scotland, as in many countries in the world, active learning is seen as an appropriate way for children to develop vital *skills and knowledge* and a positive attitude to learning (CfE, Building the Curriculum 2, p. 5).

(7) Learning across all these experiences and outcomes will enable young people to develop breadth of *knowledge and understanding and apply their skills* in a wide range of contexts (CfE, Building the Curriculum 3, p. 35).

(8) The purposes of assessment are to: support learning that develops the *knowledge and understanding, skills, attributes and capabilities* which contribute to the four capacities (CfE, Building the Curriculum 5, p. 5).

(9) Assessment will support learning and promote learner engagement resulting in greater breadth and depth in learning, including a greater focus on the secure development of *knowledge, understanding and skills* (CfE, Building the Curriculum 5, p. 7) (emphasis added).

These inconsistencies create a subtle, but pervasive sense of confusion about the purpose of curriculum – views about what actually matters and, even more importantly given the time constraints and complexities of schools and classroom, what matters most become unlikely to be shared amongst curriculum users.

Similar issues are evident in statements defining the NZC national standards; for example, there are mixed messages about what they are, which arguably, leaves those charged with implementing the policies uncertain about whether they should focus on knowledge or not. In a document outlining questions and answers about the standards, their role in outlining what students should know (alongside what they should be able to do) is made explicit. In the reading and writing standards documents, however, the knowledge purpose is much less explicit, or even absent:

They [national standards] are *descriptions of what students should know and be able to do* in reading, writing, and mathematics at different points of their schooling from years 1–8. (New Zealand Ministry of Education, 2013, emphasis not in original)

The standards *will focus the education system on foundation skills* and will link expectations about student progress and achievement to the demands of the New Zealand Curriculum. (New Zealand Ministry of Education, 2009, p. 5, emphasis not in original)

A similar misalignment is evident across two Scottish documents in statements about the experiences and outcomes of the CfE. In one, knowledge is the first in a list of aspirations that are described as being summed up by the experiences and outcomes. In the other, knowledge is absent in a description of what learning experiences should develop, whilst mention of capabilities and attributes remain:

These experiences and outcomes . . . support the progressive development of ideas, skills and ways of thinking. . .Taken together, experiences and outcomes across the curriculum areas will sum up national aspirations for every young person: the knowledge and understanding, skills, capabilities and attributes we hope they will develop. (CfE, Building the Curriculum 1, pp. 2–3)

The title 'experiences and outcomes' recognises the importance of the quality and nature of the learning *experience* in developing attributes and capabilities and in achieving active engagement, motivation and depth of learning. An *outcome* represents what is to be achieved. Taken as a whole, the experiences and outcomes embody the attributes and capabilities of the four capacities. (CfE, Experiences and Outcomes, p. 3)

Similar lack of alignment was apparent with regard to descriptions about the four capacities. In the outline of the four capacities, there is one mention of knowledge (Scottish Executive, 2004a) and that is in the text about the 'responsible citizens' capacity. It signals an aspiration for 'citizens with respect for others, commitment to participate responsibly in political, economic, social and cultural life and able to develop knowledge and understanding of the world and Scotland's place in it' (p. 12). In the Building the Curriculum 1 document that outlines the contribution to the curriculum areas to the four capacities, we examined whether there was alignment; in other words, did the detail about the contribution of each of the learning areas to the capacity of 'responsible citizens' also refer to the importance of knowledge? We found that to be the case in only two of the nine areas – mathematics and social studies:

Developing responsible citizens:

Applying mathematics in other curriculum areas helps children and young people to develop their knowledge and understanding of, for example, issues of sustainability. (Scottish Executive, 2004a, p. 19)

Through social studies children and young people gradually build up a framework of historical, geographical, social, economic and political knowledge and understanding. (Scottish Executive, 2004a, p. 35)

We suggest that these mixed messages reduce the certainty, or at least the clarity, of expectation that teachers emphasise knowledge.

Discussion

The answer to our question about whether knowledge has been downgraded is not as clear-cut as perhaps claimed by some critics, as exemplified in the quotation that precedes the paper. It can be addressed at a number of levels: through analysis of high-level statements of intent; through clarity and coherence of guidance to practitioners; and ultimately, as curriculum should be seen as practice as well as policy, in its effects in schools as those practitioners make the curriculum through their daily interactions with students.

At the highest level, we would argue knowledge continues to be a fundamental focus of aims, purposes and goals within the new curriculum, at least in the context of the NZC and CfE examined here. Disciplinary knowledge remains a purpose, and arguably one of the most the important purposes, of these curricula, and a key focus of the outcomes intended by curriculum policies.

Nonetheless, the acquisition of knowledge remains only one of a variety of purposes of education within the new curriculum, rather than the key purpose that distinguishes education from other activities, as advocated by social realists such as Young (2007). In such a context, one might therefore argue that in reducing the primacy of knowledge in the curriculum, governments are indeed downgrading knowledge. Moreover, we can add an observation here that, in both countries, there is an explicit intention that content should not be heavily prescribed, but should be flexible and subject to decision by local experts – the teachers – who are best placed to make such decisions. The desired knowledge is therefore typically expressed as broad ideas or conceptual understandings which teachers should develop using content and through contexts of their own choice. Thus, this approach to curriculum policy specifies, for example, that students should 'gain knowledge, skills and experiences to understand how cultural interaction impacts on cultures and societies' (NZC Social Studies achievement objective, Level 5). This contrasts with the National Curriculum in England, which is far more prescriptive in its specification of the content to be learned:

Pupils should be taught about:

The achievements of the earliest civilizations – an overview of where and when the first civilizations appeared and a depth study of one of the following: Ancient Sumer, The Indus Valley, Ancient Egypt, The Shang Dynasty of Ancient China.

Ancient Greece – a study of Greek life and achievements and their influence on the western world. (Department for Education, 2013, p. 208)

These high-level messages and the academic arguments about the relative importance of knowledge in the curriculum and the degree to which it should be specified are only part of the story. What seems equally important to us is our finding about mixed messages in the attention to and positioning of knowledge. Design issues (inconsistencies, lack of alignment and lack of coherence) within and across policy texts are prevalent and lead to uncertainty for those receiving and implementing such policies. School leaders and teachers are potentially left, given the design issues, uncertain about what is most important and whether they should or should not prioritise attention to developing their students' knowledge.

In our view, calls to prescribe specific content at the level of national curricula (such as those made by various social realists) are not conducive to the increasing professionalisation of teaching. Rather, such specification contributes to issues such as those described by Swann, McIntyre, Pell, Hargreaves, and Cunningham (2010) about teacher professionalism in England – a lack of trust in teachers by the public and by the government. The prominent but general indicators of the importance of knowledge in the NZC and CfE (without content specification) might be seen to signal a move away from the managerialist education policies widely critiqued in education, for their 'emphasis on efficiency and external accountability [that] treats teachers as functionaries rather than professionals and thereby diminishes their autonomy and commitment' (Codd, 2005, p. 201). Rather, the professional space for teachers to determine content, assuming their recognition of the call to give students access to knowledge, might signal a shift towards higher levels of professional trust and a greater emphasis on teacher autonomy and agency as they make the curriculum in their local contexts.[6] A further issue is the lack of specification in curriculum guidance in both countries of a process for deriving such knowledge from curricular purposes. What considerations should teachers attend to in making decisions about content? How might they determine relative importance of content to develop knowledge in various circumstances? What processes should schools have for monitoring and reviewing the approach to content? These issues are not clearly explored in either curriculum. Thus, in terms of curricular practice, there remain at least two risks. One is that schools might downgrade knowledge. The other is the risk of content being specified for the wrong reasons: purely to meet the demands of assessment, to fit with existing resources or simply to follow tradition, rather than through a process of thoughtful decisions about content that fits curricular purposes.

The influence of high-stakes assessment on teaching and learning in schools, and the role it has in narrowing the curriculum, has been the source of much criticism (Berliner, 2011). Curriculum narrowing is harmful, he says, because it 'reduces many students' chances of being thought talented in school and results in a restriction in the creative and enjoyable activities engaged in by teachers and students' (p. 287). Such criticism is unlikely to resonate with those arguing for greater emphasis on knowledge in curricula. It may, though, resonate with the call for powerful knowledge (Young & Muller, 2010), given findings such as those in a study Berliner cites, comparing Chinese and American university students (Bao et al., 2009). They were tested on their knowledge of force and their knowledge of electricity and magnetism. The Chinese students gained dramatically higher scores than their US counterparts. Their 'success' was explained by the narrowing of the curriculum (and narrowing of what constitutes knowledge in physics) due to the tyranny of high-stakes assessment. Whether such findings indicate 'success' is questionable, since the other test involved in the study was one of scientific reasoning. On this measure, arguably the most important, Chinese students did no better than the American students. The high stakes assessment and subsequent narrow curriculum seemed to have a detrimental impact in this regard.

The issue of curriculum narrowing is not confined to high-stakes assessment. An empirical examination of the effect of low-stakes exit exams reveals that teachers teach to the test, even in assessments that do not involve external examiners or severe consequences (Jäger, Marki, Oerke, & Holmeier, 2012). Even low-stakes assessment led teachers to ignore students' interests, bypass relevant current issues and narrow the curriculum.

In conclusion, we can state that both the NZC and CfE place a strong emphasis on the importance of acquiring knowledge, but they are less clear in specifying what knowledge is to be acquired or the processes which practitioners might follow in order to specify such knowledge. Moreover, analysis of the positioning of knowledge in relation to other curriculum elements in curriculum policy texts revealed mixed messages in respect of knowledge. Some features of the organisation, structure and emphasis of the texts support the claim that knowledge has been downgraded, whereas other features strongly point to a continued emphasis on knowledge, although not as the single most important curricular design aspect.

Thus, this empirical analysis partially supports the claim that these curricula have downgraded knowledge – they have greatly reduced the specification of content, de-emphasised the importance of knowledge in relation to other aspects (skills, competencies, etc.), and failed to provide explicit guidance on processes to the practitioners charged with developing them. Therefore, in spite of the strong emphasis given to knowledge in the high-level statements of intent in both curricula, they run the risk that knowledge will be downgraded in practice, through inconsistent approaches to specifying content that is then potentially not fit for curricular purpose.

Acknowledgements

The authors would like to acknowledge Frauke Meyer from the University of Auckland for her invaluable assistance with this analysis of the New Zealand's Curriculum Framework (NZCF) and CfE.

Notes

1. We note here that in at least two Anglophone countries, this trend has stuttered or even reversed; in England, following the election of a Conservative government in 2010, there has been a return to the specification of 'essential' content, inspired by E.D. Hirsch's notion of cultural literacy (see, for example, http://www.theguardian.com/education/2012/oct/15/hirsch core knowledge curriculum review); in Australia, the nascent national curriculum looks set to follow similar trends (Brennan & Zipin, 2013). This serves to remind us that curriculum policy making is an inherently political business, subject to the vagaries of local politics and concerns, as well as to global pressures and trends.
2. The article in question was reporting the award of the prize for the best paper of the year (2013) by the British Educational Research Journal to a New Zealand Academic, Elizabeth Rata, for her article 'The politics of knowledge in education (see Rata, 2012a). Rata has been extremely critical of the curricular directions taken in New Zealand and elsewhere.
3. Health and well being, languages, mathematics, science, social studies, expressive arts, technologies and religious and moral education.
4. Note that unless stated otherwise, all CfE documents are assumed to be sourced from the CfE web page at Education Scotland (Education Scotland, 2013).
5. In New Zealand there are two partner curriculum documents. The NZC in English and Te Marautanga in Maori for Maori medium schools. All references in this paper are drawn from the English medium version (New Zealand Ministry of Education, 2007).
6. For an extended discussion of whether teachers can indeed take advantage of the autonomy apparently afforded by the new curriculum, see Priestley, Biesta, and Robinson (2013).

References

Australian Council of Educational Research. (2002). *Report on the New Zealand National Curriculum*. Retrieved from http://www.educationcounts.govt.nz/publications/curriculum/5823

Bao, L., Cai, T., Koenig, L., Fang, K., Han, J., Wang, J., ... Wu, N. (2009). Physics: Learning and scientific reasoning. *Science, 323*, 586 587. doi:10.1126/science.1167740

Beane, J.A. (1997). *Curriculum integration: Designing the core of a democratic education*. New York, NY: Teachers College Press.

Berliner, D. (2011). Rational responses to high stakes testing: the case of curriculum narrowing and the harm that follows. *Cambridge Journal of Education, 41*, 287 302. doi:10.1080/0305764X.2011.607151

Bernstein, B. (1990). *The structuring of pedagogic discourse: Class codes and control* (Vol. *4*). London: Routledge.

Biesta, G.J.J. (2011, February 21). *Experience, meaning and knowledge: A pragmatist view on knowledge and the curriculum*. A paper presented at the ESRC Seminar Series, Curriculum for the 21st Century: Theory, Policy and Practice (Seminar One: Knowledge and the Curriculum), Stirling.

Biesta, G.J.J., & Priestley, M. (2013). A curriculum for the twenty-first century? In M. Priestley & G.J.J. Biesta (Eds.), *Reinventing the curriculum: New trends in curriculum policy and practice* (pp. 229 236). London: Bloomsbury.

Boyd, B. (1997). The statutory years of secondary education: Change and progress. In M.M. Clark & P. Munn (Eds.), *Education in Scotland: Policy and practice from pre-school to secondary* (pp. 52 66). London: Routledge.

Brennan, M., & Zipin, L. (2013, September 13). *National curriculum in a federation: Shelving questions about democracy and equity in Australian schooling*? Paper presented at the European Conference for Educational Research, Istanbul.

Codd, J. (2005). Teachers as 'managed professionals' in the global education industry: The New Zealand experience. *Educational Review, 57*, 193 206. doi:10.1080/00131910420003083.69

Department for Education. (2013). The national curriculum in England: Framework document. Retrieved from https://www.gov.uk/government/uploads/system/uploads/attachment data/file/210969/NC framework document - FINAL.pdf

Dewey, J. (1907). Waste in education. In J. Dewey (Ed.), *The school and society: Being three lectures by John Dewey supplemented by a statement of the University Elementary School*. Retrieved from http://www.brocku.ca/MeadProject/Dewey/Dewey 1907/Dewey 1907c.html

Ecclestone, K. (2013). Confident individuals: The implications of an 'emotional subject' for curriculum priorities and practices. In M. Priestley & G.J.J. Biesta (Eds.), *Reinventing the curriculum: New trends in curriculum policy and practice* (pp. 75 98). London: Bloomsbury.

Education Scotland. (2013). *The curriculum in Scotland*. Retrieved from http://www.educationscotland.gov.uk/thecurriculum/

Gardner, H. (1991). *The unschooled mind: How children think and schools should teach*. New York, NY: Basic Books.

Gill, S., & Thomson, G. (2012). *Rethinking secondary education: A human-centred approach*. Harlow: Pearson.

Goodson, I.F., & Marsh, C.J. (1996). *Studying school subjects: A guide*. London: Falmer Press.

Jäger, D.J., Marki, K.M., Oerke, B., & Holmeier, M. (2012). Statewide low-stakes tests and a teaching to the test effect? An analysis of teacher survey data from two German states. *Assessment in Education: Principles, Policy & Practice, 19*, 451 467. doi:10.1080/0969594X.2012.677803

Jakobi, A.P. (2012). International organisations and policy diffusion: The global norm of lifelong learning. *Journal of International Relations and Development, 15*, 31 64. doi:10.1057/jird.2010.20

Kelly, A.V. (1999). *The curriculum: Theory and practice* (4th ed.). London: Sage.

Le Métais, J. (2002). *New Zealand stocktake: An international critique*. Wellington: The Ministry of Education. Retrieved from http://www.educationcounts.govt.nz/ data/ assets/pdf file/0019/9451/nz-stocktake-an-international-critique.pdf

Minty, S., & Priestley, M. (2012). *Developing curriculum for excellence: Summary of research findings from a Scottish local authority*. Stirling: University of Stirling.

Moore, R., & Young, M. (2001). Knowledge and the curriculum in the sociology of education: Towards a reconceptualization. *British Journal of Sociology of Education, 22*, 445 461. doi:10.1080/01425690120094421

New Zealand Herald. (2013, September 7). Knowledge lost from our kids' learning: Expert. *New Zealand Herald*. Retrieved from http://www.nzherald.co.nz/nz/news/article.cfm?c id=1&objectid=11120936

New Zealand Ministry of Education. (2007). *The New Zealand Curriculum*. Wellington: Learning Media.

New Zealand Ministry of Education. (2009). *Reading and writing standards for years 1 8*. Retrieved from http://nzcurriculum.tki.org.nz/National-Standards/Reading-and-writing-standards

New Zealand Ministry of Education. (2013). *National standards questions and answers*. Retrieved from http://nzcurriculum.tki.org.nz/National-Standards/Key-information/Questions-and-answers

Nieveen, N., & Kuiper, W. (2012). Balancing curriculum and freedom in the Netherlands. *European Educational Research Journal, 11*, 357 368. doi:10.2304/eerj.2012.11.3.357

Phillips, D., & Ochs, K. (2003). Processes of policy borrowing in education: Some explanatory and analytical devices. *Comparative Education, 39*, 451 461. doi:10.1080/0305006032000162020

Pickering, M.J. (2004). Qualitative content analysis. In M.S. Lewis-Beck, A. Bryman, & T.F. Liao (Eds.), *Encyclopedia of social science research methods* (pp. 890 891). Thousand Oaks, CA: Sage.

Priestley, M. (2011). Whatever happened to curriculum theory? Critical realism and curriculum change. *Pedagogy, Culture and Society, 19*, 221 237. doi:10.1080/14681366.2011.582258

Priestley, M., Biesta, G.J.J., & Robinson, S. (2013). Teachers as agents of change: Teacher agency and emerging models of curriculum. In M. Priestley & G.J.J. Biesta (Eds.), *Reinventing the curriculum: New trends in curriculum policy and practice* (pp. 187 206). London: Bloomsbury.

Priestley, M., Robinson, S., & Biesta, G.J.J. (2012). Teacher agency, performativity and curriculum change: Reinventing the teacher in the Scottish curriculum for excellence? In B. Jeffrey & G. Troman (Eds.), *Performativity across UK education: Ethnographic cases of its effects, agency and reconstructions* (pp. 87 108). Painswick: E&E Publishing.

Rapley, T., & Jenkings, K.N. (2010). Document analysis. In P. Peterson, E. Baker, & B. McGaw (Eds.), *The international encyclopedia of education* (3rd ed., pp. 380 385). Oxford: Elsevier.

Rata, E. (2012a). The politics of knowledge in education. *British Educational Research Journal, 38*, 103 124. doi:10.1080/01411926.2011.615388

Rata, E. (2012b). *The politics of knowledge in education*. London: Routledge.

Scottish Executive. (2004a). *A curriculum for excellence: The curriculum review group*. Edinburgh: Author.

Scottish Executive. (2004b). *A curriculum for excellence: Ministerial response*. Edinburgh: Author.

Scottish Executive. (2006). *A curriculum for excellence: Progress and proposals*. Edinburgh: Author.

Sinnema, C. (2011). *Monitoring and evaluating curriculum implementation: Final evaluation report on the implementation of the New Zealand Curriculum, 2008-2010*. Wellington: New Zealand Ministry of Education.

Sinnema, C., & Aitken, G. (2013). Trends in international curriculum development. In M. Priestley & G.J.J. Biesta (Eds.), *Reinventing the curriculum: New trends in curriculum policy and practice* (pp. 141 164). London: Bloomsbury.

Swann, M., McIntyre, D., Pell, T., Hargreaves, L., & Cunningham, M. (2010). Teachers' conceptions of teacher professionalism in England in 2003 and 2006. *British Educational Research Journal, 36*, 549 571. doi:10.1080/01411920903018083

Watson, C. (2010). Educational policy in Scotland: Inclusion and the control society. *Discourse: Studies in the Cultural Politics of Education, 31*, 93 104. doi:10.1080/01596300903465443

Weber, R.P. (1990). *Basic content analysis* (2nd ed.). Newbury Park, CA: Sage.

Wheelahan, L. (2010). *Why knowledge matters in curriculum: A social realist argument*. London: Routledge.

White, J. (2011). *Exploring well-being in schools: A guide to making children's lives more fulfilling*. London: Routledge.

Whitty, G. (2010). Revisiting school knowledge: Some sociological perspectives on new school curricula. *European Journal of Education, 45*, 28 44. doi:10.1111/j.1465-3435.2009.01422.x

Yates, L., & Collins, C. (2010). The absence of knowledge in Australian curriculum reforms. *European Journal of Education, 45*, 89 101. doi:10.1111/j.1465-3435.2009.01417.x

Yates, L., Collins, C., & O'Connor, K. (2010). Curriculum in Australia: The challenges, the past and the future. In L. Yates, C. Collins, & K. O'Connor (Eds.), *Australia's curriculum dilemmas: State cultures and the big issues* (pp. 309 326). Carlton, VIC: Melbourne University Publishing.

Yates, L., & Young, M. (2010). Editorial: Globalization, knowledge and the curriculum. *European Journal of Education, 45*, 4 10. doi:10.1111/j.1465-3435.2009.01412.x

Young, M. (2007). *Bringing knowledge back in: From social constructivism to social realism in the sociology of education*. London: Routledge.

Young, M. (2008). From constructivism to realism in the sociology of the curriculum. *Review of Research in Education, 32*, 1 28. doi:10.3102/0091732x07308969

Young, M. (2009). *Alternative educational futures for a knowledge society. Socialism and education*. Retrieved from http://socialismandeducation.wordpress.com/2009/12/06/alternative-educational-futures-for-a-knowledge-society

Young, M., & Muller, J. (2010). Three educational scenarios for the future: Lessons from the sociology of knowledge. *European Journal of Education, 45*(1), 11 27.

Appendix 1. Knowledge coding framework

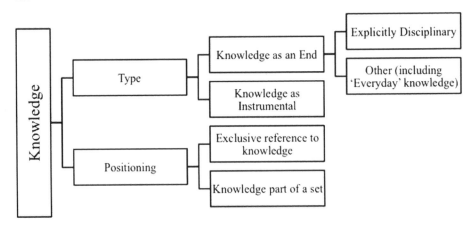

An aims-based curriculum illustrated by the teaching of science in schools

Michael J. Reiss and John White

Institute of Education, University of London, London, UK

> We begin by arguing that curriculum development should start with aims rather than, as is typically the case, with subjects. We, therefore, ask what might be the fundamental aims of school education. We conclude that they are twofold, namely, to enable each learner to lead a life that is personally flourishing and to help others to do so too. These high level aims can be translated into more specific ones by considering how human flourishing requires, for most people, such things as the acquisition of a broad background understanding, moral education, a life of imagination and reflection, and preparation for work. To illustrate our argument more specifically we then turn to the teaching of science. We show how our position relates to and simplifies present writing about the aims of science education and conclude that our proposals would result in a school science education that had similarities with much current school education, which is desirable as it suggests that our proposals are not completely unrealistic, but some non-trivial differences too, which is encouraging as it suggests that our approach has practical worth rather than simply replicating existing approaches.

Curriculum development

Curricula exist in a wide range of forms and there are a number of ways in which they can be developed (cf. Kelly, 2009). However, national curricula typically start with a list of subjects. They take for granted a dozen or so discrete school subjects and the knowledge they embody. It is subject requirements that get filled out. This has a number of consequences. For example, a subject-led curriculum, especially at secondary level, starts with, and so is necessarily constrained by, the availability of teachers capable of teaching certain subjects. More fundamentally, there is a general implicit presumption that agreement exists as to the purposes of school education without these purposes begin critically examined anew.

An alternative to starting with subjects is to start further back, with aims (Reiss & White, 2013). An aims-led curriculum has a fundamental advantage in that it can start with the needs and wants of students, both students as they live in schools and students once they have left their schooling behind. Another advantage of starting with aims is that if one doesn't, one finds that aims end up getting tagged on. For example, when the National Curriculum for England and Wales was first created in 1988, it had next to no aims to guide it. More recent versions have included lists of overall aims, but these have been tacked on to a structure already in place. Crucially, they do not *generate* that structure.

The aims of education

Some philosophers of education have argued that education would do well to have no aims. Richard Peters (1959) asked 'Must the educator have an aim?', while 40 years later Paul Standish (1999) raised the similar question 'Education without aims?' Peters took off from the thought that if a teacher really understood what 'education' means, they would not need to ask about its purposes. Indeed, it would not make sense for them to do so. Standish is also exercised by what he sees as a 'grammatical oddness' here: asking what the aims of education are is like asking about the aims of a town. There is not much sense, he thinks, in asking 'What are the aims of Aberdeen?'

Theirs seems a somewhat startling position. Can they each be suggesting that education must be or should be aimless? How then, would teachers know what to do, what direction to take? But neither Peters nor Standish is in fact suggesting absence of purpose. Peters's conception of education is so substantive – he sees it as initiation into intrinsically valuable activities to do with the pursuit of truth – that it *already* incorporates aims within itself. The issue is not whether educators need aims, but whether they need Peters's truth-seeking aim (alone) or whether other aims should come into the picture. Standish's discussion later in his essay shows that he thinks education should have to do with a spiritual ascent towards the Good (not this that can be properly put into words). His position seems to be not that aims of education do not exist, but that they are ineffable.

It is difficult to defend the notion that education should be aimless. People do design school curricula, run schools and decide how to train teachers with purposes in mind. How else could they get by? And if we look at things historically, we can see even from a cursory survey that education has been credited with diverse aims over the years. As Harris has put it:

> ... in the very first lecture of every course I give, I stress that 'education' is a changing, contested and often highly personalised, historically and politically constructed concept. To illustrate this I read a few dictionary

definitions of 'education', as well as a selected set of stated 'aims of education'. When students hear that D.H. Lawrence claimed education should aim to 'lead out the individual nature in every man and woman to its true fullness', that for Rousseau the aim of education was 'to come into accord with teaching of nature', that R.M. Hutchins saw the aim of education as 'cultivation of the intellect', that A.S. Neill believed the aim of education should be to 'make people happier, more secure, less neurotic, less prejudiced', and that John Locke claimed 'education must aim at virtue and teach man to deny his desires, inclinations and appetite, and follow as reason directs'; hopefully the penny has dropped. (Harris, 1999, p. 1)

Nevertheless, even though the examples that Harris cites have been chosen to represent their diversity, they in fact indicate considerable congruence. We can discern two broad groupings. First, those where the intention is to develop the individual for her/his own benefit; second, where the intention is to develop individuals so that they may collectively contribute to making the world a better place (Reiss, 2007). We may note that this is typical of much social policy in many countries. So, for example, in the West under-age pregnancy, illicit drug misuse and speeding are generally seen as bad both for the individuals concerned (loss of opportunities, mental and physical harm, risk of injury or death) and for the rest of society (financial cost, more burglaries, harm and upset caused to families and friends).

We can put the proposition more formally: our contention is that there are two fundamental aims of school education, namely to enable each learner to lead a life that is personally flourishing and to help others to do so too.

What constitutes a flourishing life?

In the historical West, the notion that humans should lead flourishing lives is among the oldest of ethical principles, one that is emphasised particularly by Aristotle in his *Nicomachean Ethics* and *Politics*. There are many accounts as to what precisely constitutes a flourishing life. A hedonist sees it in terms of maximising pleasurable feelings and minimising painful ones. More everyday perspectives may tie it to wealth, fame, consumption or, more generally, satisfying one's major desires, whatever these may be. Admittedly, there are difficulties with all these accounts (White, 2011). A problem besetting desire satisfaction is that it allows ways of life that virtually all of us would deny were flourishing, a life wholly devoted to spread betting, for instance.

A life filled with whole-hearted and successful involvement in more worthwhile pursuits – such things as significant relationships, meaningful work, painting, scholarly research or enjoying a hobby, gardening, cooking, watching excellent films – is on a different plane. Virtually all of us would rate it fulfilling. At the same time, nearly all of us in a modern society like our own presume it is largely up to us to choose the mix of relationships and activities that best suits us (certain family obligations are generally excepted from this generalisation, though less than in the past). Unlike many of our ancestors, nearly all of us are deeply attached to personal autonomy as a value and feel that we have a right to this attachment.

A central aim of the school should, therefore, be to prepare students for a life of autonomous, whole-hearted and successful engagement in worthwhile relationships, activities and experiences. With many of these – cooperative work activity, friendships and enjoying literature, for instance – it makes good sense to see that students gain first-hand experience. For others – things like mountaineering, composing symphonies, choosing to live an unmarried life, running a multinational company – imagined rather than direct involvement is likely to be more appropriate. This aim also involves acquainting students with a wide range of possible options from which to choose. With their development towards autonomous adulthood in mind, schools should provide students with increasing opportunities to choose among the pursuits that best suit them. Young children are likely to need greater guidance from their teachers, just as they do from their parents. Part of the function of schooling, and indeed parenting, is to prepare children for the time when they will need to, and be able to, make decisions more independently. In school, whether curriculum activities are chosen by students or presented to them without choice, the intention should be that students whole-heartedly and enjoyably immerse themselves in them.

Equipping every student to help others to lead personally fulfilling lives

We want children to want other people, as well as themselves, to lead fulfilling lives. Negatively, this means not hurting them, not lying to them, not breaking one's word or in other ways impeding them in this. Positively, it means helping them to reach their goals, respecting their autonomy and being fair, friendly and cooperative in one's dealings with them. Schools can reinforce and extend what parents and others in families do in developing morality in children. Schools can widen students' moral sensitivity beyond the domestic circle to those in other communities, locally, nationally and globally. They can also help them to think about moral conflicts in their own lives and in the wider spheres just mentioned. They can encourage students to reflect on the basis of morality, including whether this is religious or non-religious.

As part of their moral education, schools should help students to become informed and active citizens of a liberal democratic society. Dispositionally, this means encouraging them to take an interest in political affairs at local, national and global levels from the standpoint of a concern for the general good; and to do this with due regard to framework values of liberal democracy such as freedom, individual autonomy, equal consideration and cooperation. Young people also need to possess whatever sorts of understanding these dispositions entail, e.g. an understanding of the nature of liberal democracy in general, of divergences of opinion about it, and of its application to the circumstances of their own society.

As future citizens, the great majority of students will contribute to the general well-being, as well as to their own, through work. This will often be remunerated, though much of it, e.g. caring for children or elderly relatives, may not be. As autonomous beings, students will eventually have to make choices about what kind of work to engage in. Schools should be helping them in this by making them aware of a wide range of vocational possibilities and routes into them, as well as their advantages and disadvantages.

Broad background understanding

There is an important link between the two major aims. Whatever we do in our lives that brings us personal benefit or is intended to benefit others takes place against a broad background of thoughts about the world we live in. Closest to home are thoughts about what sort of beings we are. We all grow up to believe, for instance, that we will live at most for a century or so; that we may or may not stay healthy; that the future has a considerable element of unpredictability. We all come to see our lives as inextricably bound up with the lives of other human beings. These perceptions alone cannot influence the way we lead our lives.

Part of the task of education – at home and at school – is to help students to form this background that will colour everything they do. At a fundamental level, some of us will live by religious or other beliefs that give us answers to the deep questions, while others will live without such beliefs. But much of the background is less contested. Indeed, much of it will consist of well-founded scientific conclusions – about, for instance, the social nature of human beings, our part in the ecology of nature, about the movement of planets and the building blocks of life. This leads into the second part of this article, where we explore what an aims-based approach to curriculum design might mean for education about the sciences in school. We begin by reviewing current attempts to formulate aims for school science education.

Current attempts to formulate aims for school science education

There are a multiplicity of aims for school science education (Reiss, 2007) though these are often implicit. A frequent aim of many science courses has been for them to provide a preparatory education for the small proportion of individuals who will become future scientists (in the commonly understood sense as employed professionals). This aim has been widely critiqued on democratic grounds (e.g. Millar & Osborne, 1998). After all, what of the great majority of school students who will not become such scientists?

Another aim is to enable 'scientific literacy'. Although there has been a long-running debate as to the meaning of the term (e.g. Miller, 1983), generally scientific literacy is seen as a vehicle to help tomorrow's adults to understand scientific issues (Gräber & Bolte, 1997). The basic notion is that science education should aim to enhance understanding of key ideas about the nature and practice of science as well as some of the central conclusions reached by science. Perhaps to be included within this category is the argument that to be an educated person in the twenty-first century is to understand something of science (e.g. Shamos, 1995). This is the 'science as culture' argument; that science is as worth studying *in itself*, as are, for example, literature and the arts.

A further aim is that many science courses hope that as a result of what is learnt, pupils both now and in the future, as adults, will be able to gain *practical* benefit from it. At its most straightforward this might be by entering paid employment that draws on what they have learnt in science. Although, as noted above, most students do not enter such careers they too may still benefit individually from their school science. For example, in most science courses, in countries round the world, it has long been accepted that one of the justifications for the inclusion of certain topics is that knowledge and understanding of them can promote human health. Such topics may include infectious diseases, diet, reproduction and contraception, exercise and the use of drugs (including smoking and alcohol).

Another, more mundane, way in which school science might help individual advancement is by providing what has been termed 'science education for consumerism' (Reiss, 2007). This is the hope that school science education might, for example, help us choose the most appropriate technological goods (is it worth my paying $x\%$ more for a washing machine that uses $y\%$ less hot water?). This is a sub-set of the more general argument that science education should be for public understanding (American Association for the Advancement of Science, 1990; Millar, 1996).

A further aim of school science education is that it should facilitate democracy. Longbottom and Butler (1999) argue that:

> If citizens have some knowledge of the natural world and of the process of gaining that knowledge, then they may be empowered to view critically the social world. Citizens who are critically minded, and who can analyze and challenge social structures, will be better able to implement democratic ideals. In this way, science education, in combination with a general education that teaches democratic ideals, can play a valuable part in equipping citizens with knowledge for action. (Longbottom & Butler, 1999, p. 489)

The argument that school science education should promote democracy is related to the argument that it should be for citizenship (Jenkins, 1999). In both cases, there is what has been termed a 'weak version' and a 'strong version' (Reiss, 2007). The weak versions consist of learning about what a democracy is and what it is to be a citizen. The strong versions entail using such knowledge in action to bring about change. These strong versions are closely allied to claims that the aim of school science education should be to effect social justice or socio-political action.

For example, Calabrese Barton has worked with homeless children in the USA to develop more appropriate science learning. She has shown that active participation in science lessons, and real learning about science, take place when children believe that their work can bring about improvements for themselves, their friends and their families (Calabrese Barton, 2001). She draws on feminist approaches to show that many of the students with whom she and her colleagues worked, whilst seen in school at poor attainers in science, were actually perfectly capable of high-quality science work, provided they were given real choice in the science they worked at.

It is evident that there are currently diverse aims for school science education. It is important, though, to emphasise that most teaching of school science proceeds on the assumption that such knowledge is good for students, without the precise aims having been thought through with any rigour and without the science curriculum beginning from such aims. Instead, science curricula generally begin with science. It might be thought that this is a sensible starting point but it leads all too often to disengagement as many students fail to understand the point of what they are learning (Reiss, 2000; Schreiner, 2006). In the next and final section, we outline how an aims-based approach to the curriculum might inform science education.

An aims-based approach to education about the sciences in school

School science, worldwide, is privileged in the curriculum. So far as we are aware, the school curricula of all countries have science as a mandatory, core subject to be taught, typically, from the start of schooling (e.g. 5 or 6 years of age) up to the end of compulsory schooling (e.g. 15 or 16 years of age). Whilst what precisely is included within 'science' varies a bit from country to country, and while it isn't always called 'science' for younger pupils, the presence of school science is nearly always accepted as a given. Furthermore, what gets included within the school science curriculum in typically determined mainly by curriculum history – i.e. what has previously been included – and by occasional battles; for instance, in England and Wales, about the extent to which the earth sciences should be included within science, within geography, or omitted from the school curriculum.

The argument of our *An Aims-based Curriculum* (2013) is that school education should equip every student:

- to lead a life that is personally flourishing,
- to help others to do so, too.

As discussed above, for these two aims to be realised, we add a third, the area of 'background understanding' – the understanding of human nature, of our social life and how it has developed as it is, and of the natural world in which we live. It is partly in its contribution to our background understanding that science begins to assert its case for inclusion in the school curriculum.

Our own society, unlike most in the past, is partly shaped by science. As a result, much of our background consists of presumptions about which there is little or no reasonable doubt: the belief that the Earth goes round the Sun, for instance, rather than vice versa and that germs that can cause illness come from pre-existing germs rather than from 'bad air' (malaria) or elsewhere.

More fundamentally, students need to be helped to understand their own nature and that of other people as human beings. This has a biological aspect: they need to understand something of how they function biologically, and also how they are connected with the rest of the living world. Some grasp of evolutionary theory, genetics and child development is essential here. But there is also a cultural aspect: human beings, as language users, are the only animals (setting aside the beginnings of self-consciousness seen in a few other species) known to be conscious of their own existence. Students need to be inducted into the implications of this for our social life, including its forms of cooperation and its intellectual and artistic achievements.

Notice here how difficult it is to pigeon-hole knowledge into discrete school subjects. In England, in response to the view that biology at advanced level (for 16- to 18-year-olds) was rather narrow in its focus, apparently being aimed principally at students hoping to study it or another science at university, the subject 'social biology' was devised as an alternative. It went considerably beyond normal biology in an attempt to produce a richer account of what it is to be human and was supported not by a single textbook but by a series of short topic books with such titles as *Behaviour and Social Organisation* (Reiss & Sants, 1987), *Environmental Concerns* (Alma, 1993), *Drugs, Alcohol and Human Health* (Cornwell & Cornwell, 1993) and *The Origins of Humankind* (Tomkins, 1998).

Students' scientific background will also include elementary astronomical knowledge of the place of the Earth and other planets in our solar system, and of the relation of that system to the wider universe. It will also take them into what is known about how the universe operates, its fundamental constituents at molecular, atomic and sub-atomic levels, its chemical composition and the basic forces that direct it. Evolutionary perspectives are also central to students' understanding of the living world of animal and plant life within its varying geographical and geological contexts.

Although this aim embraces the transmission of much knowledge, not least scientific knowledge, this is always in the service of helping students to build up a background. Big ideas are more important in this than specifics (Harlen, 2010), and accumulating knowledge is in the interests of reflection on and discussion about the bigger picture that is being put together.

As far as the sciences go, perhaps above all they help us to situate ourselves both temporally and spatially in the world in which we live. It is clear that the universe is almost unimaginably old – some 13.7 billion years is the current consensus – and that there are literally many billions of stars, a high proportion of them with planets of their own. In one sense then science tells us that our own world is not that special. And yet we still do not know whether our planet alone is home to life.

Science proceeds through the objective testing of hypotheses about our material world. The growth in scientific knowledge gives us greater understanding of that world. Thanks to science, there is, for instance, no need for people to be superstitious or to fear witchcraft. Tsunamis and infectious diseases – still, sadly, all too often with attendant human misery and loss of life – are not the result of individual wickedness.

School coverage of the sciences should therefore include something about what is generally referred to as 'the nature of science', i.e. how scientific knowledge is arrived at and its limits (Kind & Kind, 2008; Williams, 2011). For example, science tells us much about why the world is as it is, not what we should do in it. If we want students to know something of the ethical implications of science, we either have to admit the teaching of ethics within science or arrange for such teaching to occur elsewhere in the curriculum. More generally, teaching about the methods of science and the nature of science can help learners appreciate that while much scientific knowledge is robust – one thinks of ideas such as matter is particulate or that inherited traits result in large measure from the specific coding sequences of nucleic acids – it is always provisional so that there is always the possibility of change. A paradigmatic instance of this is the replacement of Newtonian physics some 250 years later by a blend of relativity and quantum theory.

In addition, certain core scientific material should be included: the particulate theory of matter, the difference between elements, atoms and molecules, the germ origins of much disease, the evidence for evolution, the importance of natural selection, the way in which the structures of organisms are related to how they function, the interrelationships between organisms and their environments, the relationship between electricity and magnetism, certain basic laws of physics such as the conservation of mass, the conservation of energy and the second law of thermodynamics, the importance of gravitational and other forces, the role of plate tectonics. Such knowledge is said to be 'powerful' (cf. Young, 2008, 2013; and for a critique White, 2012).

However, when deciding what material should be included within a curriculum, the criterion of background understanding is not enough. As we argued above, the great majority of students will contribute to the general well-being, as well as to their own, through work. While mathematics and technology have been around for millennia and 'modern' science for at least several hundred years, it is clear that the proportion of jobs that rely on these subjects has increased in recent decades. Indeed, it seems to be the endless lament of Western governments that we aren't producing enough university STEM (science, technology, engineering and mathematics) graduates (European Commission, 2004; National Academy of Sciences, 2007).

Of course, it is difficult to predict if such shortages of STEM graduates (and others who work in STEM fields, e.g. as technicians) will continue. Perhaps increasing developments in automation will mean that many STEM jobs will no longer exist just as, in past times, first agricultural and then industrial employment rose and fell. Nevertheless, STEM graduates are presently in short supply in many countries (as evidenced by the higher earnings they typically obtain once in post).

How, though, should one decide, for such possible employment purposes, how much and what sort of science students should experience when at school? The first principle, surely, should be to provide sufficient material for students to be reasonably well informed when deciding whether or not to continue with the subject for career reasons once it becomes optional. This does not point to a compulsory science curriculum, providing comprehensive coverage; science teaching could include, among other things, what we refer to as 'taster-option' courses (Reiss & White, 2013). Furthermore, a significant proportion of this material should be 'applied' so as to indicate the uses to which such knowledge is put. Indeed, not only should it be applied but courses should indicate how people make use of it in employment.

To give just one example, when teaching the topic of memory, say when teaching the nervous system to 13-year-olds, one might include material on how such knowledge is used by nurses who help people who have Alzheimer's disease, by cognitive behavioural therapists who work with people who have obsessive compulsive disorder, by dog handlers who train dogs to act in films, by teachers attempting to enable their students to learn and understand and by students when revising.

However, despite attempts to introduce more applied material into a number of science courses, such material, and not only in science courses, is often considered of lower intellectual worth than 'pure' knowledge (Pring et al., 2009). Such an attitude, aside from being narrow-minded, is probably counterproductive; some students are attracted by learning material that they can see might lead to satisfying employment. In any event, the relationship between pure and applied science is not simply a one way one in which pure knowledge leads to applied knowledge. As historians and sociologists of science now accept, the relationship is more complicated than that. In some cases, advances in the applied sciences lead to advances in pure sciences (Ziman, 2000).

By now it might be objected that what we are proposing for science is not that different from what it often taught in science nowadays. To this we respond in three ways. First, would that this were the case. In our experience, too often science teaching does not give due consideration to its aims or to the interests of all its learners, instead serving up a fare that appeals to the tastes of only a minority of those required to consume it. Second, some similarity with what currently sometimes takes place in science classrooms is encouraging, as it suggests that our proposals are not unrealistic. Third, there are a number of ways in which a science curriculum that starts with aims would be likely to differ from one that starts with what is typically taught. We will give two concluding examples.

First, we have not argued that there must be an equal representation of biology, chemistry and physics at each age and in every school year, whereas this seems to be implicit presumption of much curriculum debate in science education, certainly in England. However, it can be argued that the amount of chemistry and physics that needs to be taught in primary schools is rather small. Much of these subjects is quite abstract and difficult not only for pupils to learn but for teachers to teach. For example, some primary curricula require pupils to be able to show the direction in which forces act on objects and to appreciate the implications for motion when forces are not balanced. Yet we know (diSessa, 1993) that quite a high proportion of physics graduates find it difficult consistently to apply Newton's first (If there is no net force on an object, then it continues in a straight line at constant speed) and third (When a first body exerts a force $\mathbf{F}_1$ on a second body, the second body simultaneously exerts a force $\mathbf{F}_2$ on the first body equal to $-\mathbf{F}_1$) laws of motion, let alone truly to have internalised them.

Second, a curriculum that takes seriously human flourishing will give more weight to certain science topics and less to others than the present curriculum does. For most of us, sex and relationships education is more important than magnets, balancing chemical equations or the structure of prokaryotes. Before it is objected that sex and relationships education need not take place in school science lessons, as distinct from elsewhere in the curriculum, we entirely concur. One of our central points is that schools should be left free, within a relatively substantive overall national aims framework, to decide how and where to teach whatever best promotes these aims.

In the case of sex and relationship education, two points can be made. First, there is far more to successful learning in this area than simply the acquisition of knowledge; there are skills to be acquired and dispositions to be formed (Halstead & Reiss, 2003). Second, there is quite a bit that might end up conventionally within the purview of schools science. For example, the way we teach sex and sexuality in school science is far too oversimplified. For a start, not everyone is simply XX or XY. And then there is the fact that chromosomal sex doesn't exactly correspond to how people see themselves. In a typical secondary school with over a thousand students, there are likely to be half a dozen or more who don't fit neatly into the binary classification of male is XY, female is XX. And when it comes to teaching about sexuality there is, of course, far more diversity than most school biology textbooks seem comfortable admitting (Reiss, 1998).

More generally, our argument is that when the aims of education take precedence, then what is taught and how it is taught will shift. Education undergoes something of a Gestalt switch in which things are seen differently and this permits teachers to teach with new emphases. We have outlined how this might occur for science education but our point holds more broadly. Our hope is that subject specialists may be persuaded by our argument – or at least be willing to explore its implications. At the very least, our approach will allow teachers to give rather more satisfying answers to the familiar question 'Why do we have to learn this sir/miss?' than is presently often the case.

References

Alma, P. (1993). *Environmental concerns*. Cambridge: Cambridge University Press.

American Association for the Advancement of Science. (1990). *Science for all Americans: Project 2061*. New York, NY: Oxford University Press.

Calabrese Barton, A. (2001). Science education in urban settings: Seeking new ways of praxis through critical ethnography. *Journal of Research in Science Teaching, 38*, 899 917.

Cornwell, A., & Cornwell, V. (1993). *Drugs, alcohol and human health*. Cambridge: Cambridge University Press.

diSessa, A.A. (1993). Toward an epistemology of physics. *Cognition and Instruction, 10*, 105 225.

European Commission. (2004). *Europe needs more scientists: Report by the high level group on increasing human resources for science and technology*. Brussels: Author.

Gräber, W., & Bolte, C. (Eds.). (1997). *Scientific literacy: An international symposium IPN 154*. Kiel: Institut für die Pädagogik der Naturwissenschaften an der Universitatät Kiel.

Halstead, J.M., & Reiss, M.J. (2003). *Values in sex education: From principles to practice*. London: RoutledgeFalmer.

Harlen, W. (Ed.). (2010). *Principles and big ideas of science education*. Hatfield: Association for Science Education. Retrieved from http://www.ase.org.uk/documents/principles-and-big-ideas-of-science-education/.

Harris, K. (1999). Aims! Whose aims? In R. Marples, (Ed.), *The aims of education* (pp. 1 13). London: Routledge.

Jenkins, E.W. (1999). School science, citizenship and the public understanding of science. *International Journal of Science Education, 21*, 703 710.

Kelly, A.V. (2009). *The curriculum: Theory and practice* (6th ed.). Los Angeles, CA: Sage.

Kind, V., & Kind, P.M. (2008). *Teaching secondary how science works*. London: John Murray.

Longbottom, J.E., & Butler, P.H. (1999). Why teach science? Setting rational goals for science education. *Science Education, 83*, 473 492.

Miller, J. (1983). Scientific literacy: a conceptual and empirical review. *Daedalus, 112*(2), 29 48.

Millar, R. (1996). Towards a science curriculum for public understanding. *School Science Review, 77*(280), 7 18.

Millar, R., & Osborne, J. (Eds.). (1998). *Beyond 2000: Science education for the future*. London: Nuffield Foundation.

National Academy of Sciences. (2007). *Rising above the gathering storm: Energizing and employing America for a brighter economic future*. Washington, DC: The National Academies Press.

Peters, R.S. (1959). Must an educator have an aim? In R.S. Peters (Ed.), *Authority, responsibility and education* (pp. 83 95). London: Allen and Unwin.

Pring, R., Hayward, G., Hodgson, A., Johnson, J., Keep, E., Oancea, A., ... Wilde, S. (2009). *Education for all: The future of education and training for 14 19 year olds*. Abingdon: Routledge.

Reiss, M.J. (1998). The representation of human sexuality in some science textbooks for 14 16 year-olds. *Research in Science & Technological Education, 16*, 137 149.

Reiss, M.J. (2000). *Understanding science lessons: Five years of science teaching*. Buckingham: Open University Press.

Reiss, M.J. (2007). What should be the aim(s) of school science education? In D. Corrigan, J. Dillon, & R. Gunstone (Eds.), *The re-emergence of values in science education* (pp. 13 28). Rotterdam: Sense.

Reiss, M.J., & Sants, H.K.A. (1987). *Behaviour and social organization*. Cambridge: Cambridge University Press.

Reiss, M.J., & White, J. (2013). *An aims-based curriculum: The significance of human flourishing for schools*. London: IOE Press.

Schreiner, C. (2006). *Exploring a ROSE-Garden: Norwegian youth's orientations towards science seen as signs of late modern identities*. Oslo: Faculty of Education, University of Oslo.

Shamos, M.H. (1995). *The myth of scientific literacy*. New Brunswick, NJ: Rutgers University Press.

Standish, P. (1999). Education without aims? In R. Marples (Ed.), *The aims of education* (pp. 35 49). London: Routledge.

Tomkins, S. (1998). *The origins of humankind* (2nd ed.). Cambridge: Cambridge University Press.

White, J. (2011). *Exploring well-being in schools: A guide to making children's lives more fulfilling*. London: Routledge.

White, J. (2012). Powerful knowledge: Too weak a prop for the traditional curriculum? New Visions for Education Group. Retrieved from http://www.newvisionsforeducation.org.uk/2012/05/14/powerful-knowledge-too-weak-a-prop-for-the-traditional-curriculum/

Williams, J.D. (2011). *How science works: Teaching and learning in the science classroom*. London: Continuum.

Young, M.F.D. (2008). *Bringing knowledge back in: From social constructivism to social realism in the sociology of education*. London: Routledge.

Young, M. (2013). Overcoming the crisis in curriculum theory: A knowledge-based approach. *Journal of Curriculum Studies, 45*(2), 101 118.

Ziman, J. (2000). *Real science: What it is, and what it means*. Cambridge: Cambridge University Press.

Two contrasting Australian Curriculum responses to globalisation: what students should learn or become

Bob Lingard[a] and Glenda McGregor[b]

[a]School of Education, The University of Queensland, Brisbane, Australia; [b]School of Education and Professional Studies, Griffith University, Brisbane, Australia

> This paper compares two contrasting educational policy responses to globalisation in Australia: the 'New Basics' experiment that occurred in the State of Queensland (2000–2003) and the Australian Curriculum, which is currently being implemented across the nation from preschool to Year 10 in English, history, mathematics and science. These initiatives illustrate the tensions that have continued to mount during the last decade over answers to the question of 'what counts' as the most valuable knowledge and/or skills needed to negotiate the complexities of a rapidly globalising world. Illustrating one international trend of favouring the development of competencies and dispositions, the New Basics project abandoned traditional school subjects for futures oriented, 'real-world' learning. The Australian Curriculum demonstrates a strong return to 'the disciplines', partly as a local backlash against experiments like the New Basics and Outcomes Based Education, but also motivated by the desire to improve the nation's performance on international tests; however, via its framework of 'cross-curriculum priorities' and 'general capabilities', the Australian Curriculum also pays heed to the rhetoric of shaping the individual as the kind of person with the skills and dispositions required by the global millennium citizen and worker.

Curriculum defines what counts as valid knowledge, pedagogy defines what counts as valid transmission of knowledge, and evaluation defines what counts as a valid realization of the knowledge on the part of the taught. (Bernstein, 1973, p. 85)

…differences within and change in the organization, transmission and evaluation of educational knowledge should be a major area of sociological interest. (Bernstein, 1971, p. 47)

Introduction

The two quotes from Bernstein at the head of this paper are demonstrative of the sociological approach to curriculum that we take (Whitty, 2010). We recognise the politics of curriculum construction, the selective tradition of curriculum and how its construction affects the other 'message systems', namely pedagogy and assessment (Bernstein, 1971). We would also argue that in contemporary education the evaluation message system, framed as high-stakes census testing, potentially affects both curriculum and pedagogy in reductive ways (Lingard, Martino, & Rezai-Rashti, 2013). In particular, the second Bernstein quote draws the sociologist's attention to the symbiotic relationships between changes in the message systems and broader social changes. We have heeded this point in the analysis provided of two Australian Curriculum responses to globalisation: the New Basics in the State of Queensland and the post-2007 move towards an Australian national curriculum. Furthermore, these responsive curriculum developments work with two common responses across the globe today in curriculum reform. One is a response that gives emphasis to the competencies and dispositions of those graduating from schooling as the way to construct the knowledge that constitutes the curriculum; the other is a return to a more traditional, discipline-based approach to constructing curricula.

The New Basics experiment was of the former kind, working with an account of the imagined future worker, citizen and person that schooling ought to produce in the rapidly changing, globalising, digitised world of the present. The Australian Curriculum, at one level at least, is a case of the discipline response to curriculum reform. However, the latter classification of the Australian Curriculum is complicated by the fact that it also gives priority to two other elements that cut across the discipline-based curriculum. These are 'cross-curriculum priorities' and 'general capabilities'. Additionally, we argue the introduction in 2008 of the National Assessment Plan – Literacy and Numeracy (NAPLAN), whereby every student in Years 3, 5, 7 and 9 is tested in May each year on literacy and numeracy, has also affected the enactment of the Australian Curriculum by using up valuable teaching time in preparing students for these tests. Whilst NAPLAN is considered low-stakes assessment for students, as a systems' accountability measure it has evolved as high stakes for systems, teachers and schools (Lingard & Sellar, 2013).

We begin with consideration of the backdrops to the development of the national curriculum and the New Basics. The specifics of the development of the New Basics in Queensland are then adumbrated, concentrating specifically on the rise and fall of this curriculum reform project. This is followed by consideration of the national policy agenda, including creation of the national curriculum and its impact upon policy reforms in

Queensland schooling. Here we show how stress on NAPLAN performance and the more discipline-based Australian Curriculum, P-10, mark a new policy moment in Queensland and Australian schooling. We acknowledge that the Australian Curriculum focuses on both what students should learn (the discipline base) and what they should become (cross-curriculum priorities and general capabilities). Our analysis of current trends in the Australian Curriculum, however, reveals these somewhat fraught attempts to marry disciplinary rigour with the shaping of capabilities and the development of trans-disciplinary knowledge and skills; an attempt to conjoin curriculum rationales of what students ought to learn with what students ought to become. Throughout, we document the global contexts of these recent curriculum reforms in Queensland and nationally.

Backdrops to the national curriculum and the New Basics

All stages and elements of the national curriculum have been mediated by Australia's federal political structure. What we see are complex mediations of national school reform flowing from the federal political structure, where schooling is ostensibly the constitutional responsibility of the states and territories (Lingard, 2000). This is evident in the reality that all elements of the Australian Curriculum as they are developed have to be approved by the intergovernmental council in education, consisting of all education ministers. This has seen an incremental staged implementation with the focus in the first instance on P-10 (5–15 year olds) curriculum and on English, mathematics, science and history. The political persuasion of these various governments is a factor in the extent of agreement, but other factors also mediate its enactment. When federal Labor began this development in 2007, all state and territory governments were Labor. The federal government is now conservative, along with that of Western Australia, Victoria, New South Wales, Queensland and the Northern Territory leaving only Tasmania, South Australia and the Australian Capital Territory (ACT) in the Labor camp.

Historically, federal Labor governments have been more centralist, while conservative governments have been more federalist. An earlier move towards a national curriculum that occurred under the Hawke and Keating Labor governments (1983–1996) was also heavily mediated by the politics of Australian educational federalism. We note, though, that both the earlier Labor moves toward a national curriculum and the more recent Rudd/Gillard one proffered globalisation as a necessary justification of the need for national approach. The centralist/federalist binary remains the case with the important difference being that the current conservative Prime Minister and government are also committed to a national curriculum and testing, but with weaker central accountability requirements of the independent and Catholic school sectors. Indeed in respect of testing, they are committed to including science testing nationally in the near future. We would argue this bipartisanship reflects the reworking of the nation in the context of globalisation and the human capital framing of education policy, or what we might see as the economisation of education policy (Rizvi & Lingard, 2010). The federal government is responsible for the 'national' economy and thus with the economistic reframing of education policy has taken a stronger role in schooling, including in curriculum. This rationale is explicitly stated in national curriculum documentation.

Federalism thus mediates the development of the Australian Curriculum and certainly has real impact on its enactment, with each of the jurisdictions putting in place different implementation time frames and mediating the national to varying degrees by state developments. For example, New South Wales has embedded the national curriculum in its own new curriculum, while Queensland is implementing in full the national curriculum and legislating so that the State has limited responsibility for P-10 curriculum. We would note that the use of 'national' in the politics of Australian schooling is a signifier of just such federal mediations. We stress, though, that until the concerted efforts towards a national curriculum during the federal Labor period (2007–2013), and earlier moves under the Hawke and Keating federal Labor governments (1983–1996), curriculum remained basically the jurisdiction of curriculum authorities in the states and territories, as did assessment and tertiary selection. Indeed, apart from national literacy and numeracy testing, assessment and reporting of the national curriculum remain the jurisdiction of the states.

Since the 1970s, the Australian State of Queensland has had a unique system of senior secondary assessment and tertiary selection based on school-based, teacher-moderated assessment. This system is currently being reviewed by the Newman conservative government elected in 2013. From the late 1990s, under State Labor governments, Queensland also saw a plethora of progressive changes and reforms in schooling at other levels of primary and lower secondary schooling. Research and academic thinking were the central elements of this renaissance. The Queensland School Reform Longitudinal Study (QSRLS) (Lingard et al., 2001), was commissioned by a Conservative State government, but adopted by a Labor government to frame reform. This research developed the concept of productive pedagogies after observing and mapping pedagogies in 1000 lessons and found there was not enough intellectual demand, connectedness or working with difference in classroom pedagogies (Lingard, 2007). The research hypothesised that this was an effect of a stress on content coverage of curriculum and insufficient awareness in respect of issues of differences in the classroom, including culture-based differences around ethnicity and indigeneity. However, the productive pedagogies research found that teachers were very caring. The empirically derived model suggested that pedagogies that were intellectually demanding, connected, supportive, and worked with and valued differences would make a difference to the learning of all students (Hayes, Mills, Christie, & Lingard, 2006). The research, following Bernstein, also argued the necessity of aligning the three message systems, an insight that underpinned the New Basics development.

Subsequent to the QSRLS, Professor Allan Luke, a researcher on the QSRLS and Head of the School of Education at The University of Queensland, was seconded as Deputy Director General to the State department and given a remit to rethink schooling, in the context of the QSRLS and particularly in relation to the re-alignment of curriculum, pedagogy and assessment in Queensland classrooms. This led to the 'New Basics' trial, which developed a new curriculum for schooling from Years 1–9 to be aligned with productive pedagogies and assessment practices called 'rich tasks'.

The rich tasks were geared to ensure high intellectual demand in pedagogies and assessment practices. These tasks were addressed collaboratively between students and at certain school junctures required public presentations to school and community members. The New Basics was about aligning curriculum, pedagogy and assessment, and recognising that investment in teachers and their professional knowledge and skills was central to enhancing learning outcomes for all students across primary and secondary schools; and, importantly, for achieving more socially just outcomes across schools serving different socio-economic and indigenous communities. The New Basics was also about what was deemed to be the central 'future-oriented' knowledge domains, dispositions and capabilities, thought necessary to twenty-first-century future set in the context of globalisation. Globalisation is spoken about in New Basics documentation as both its context and rationale, simultaneously a response to, and an expression of, globalisation in school curriculum reform. This was thus a curriculum reform based, not on disciplines, but rather on the imagined future worker and citizen in a global context.

The New Basics was an example of the type of curriculum emerging at this time around the globe and had quite a bit in common with, for example, Scotland's Curriculum for Excellence aimed at producing 'successful learners, confident individuals, responsible citizens and effective contributors' (see Priestley & Biesta, 2013; Wyse et al., 2012). These sentiments were echoed in different words in the New Basics and interestingly were reproduced exactly in both Stage 3 and Stage 4 of the English National Curriculum and in the second goal for Australian schools expressed in the Melbourne Declaration (2008), examples of travelling policy (Williams, Gannon, & Sawyer, 2013). Biesta and Priestley (2013, p. 36) describe such curriculum rationales as focusing on what the school learner should *become*, as opposed to discipline-based approaches which focus on what students should *learn*. The New Basics was developed out of a specific research project; it was explicit about its theoretical framings, especially Dewey; it dealt with pedagogy and assessment, in addition to curriculum; it was a reform or trial in about 50 schools, not implemented across the system; it was only trialled in Queensland, not nationally; it was strongly supported in its implementation through government-funded critical friends in each of the schools; and it was subject to an ongoing research gaze.

In one sense, the New Basics could be seen as a re-articulation of a progressive approach in the context of globalisation with rapid economic and social change, framed to some extent by new technologies and related multi-literacies. The New Basics experiment thus exemplifies one strand in educational thinking that posits a response to globalisation that requires schooling to shape the dispositions and skills of 'the person in the world', the millennium worker and citizen, perhaps even, the new 'cosmopolitan' (see for example, Gee, 1999; McLeod & Yates, 2006; Robbins, 1998). This was an attempt to construct the future. As Lyotard (1991) notes, 'If one wants to control a process, the best way of doing so is to subordinate the present to what is (still) called the future, since in these conditions, the future will be completely pre-determined and the present itself will cease opening onto an uncertain and contingent afterwards' (p. 65).

Internationally, this kind of approach has been criticised as further entrenching social disadvantage because of a lack of disciplinary knowledge as a context for learning. Young (2011), for example, argues that national and international trends in curriculum construction towards 'generic' curricula organised around 'capabilities' and 'dispositions' are potentially empty of meaningful content, leading to what Biesta (2012) refers to as the 'learnification' of education:

> The educational demand is not that students learn but that they learn something and that they do so for particular reasons ...the discourse of learning only becomes an educational discourse when we ask questions about the content and purpose of learning – the learning 'of what' and 'for what'. (p. 583, original emphasis)

Such concerns about the nature of the content of schooling subjects became a part of the political debate in Australia during the first decade of the twenty-first century. Signalling his support for a traditionally oriented, discipline-based subject, conservative Prime Minister John Howard, for example, called for 'a root and branch' renewal of the content and ways of teaching Australian history (Grattan, 2006).

Thus, by the end of 2007, with the election of the Rudd Labor government federally, there was considerable momentum for introduction of a more tightly controlled, discipline-based Australian Curriculum; accompanying it, however, as a result of ongoing perceptions that educationally Australia's young were falling behind their international counterparts, came a national accountability agenda with national testing of literacy and numeracy via NAPLAN. The latter is taken by all students nationally in all schools at Years 3, 5, 7 and 9.

In a sense, the national reform agenda in Australia, pursued by Labor after 2007 through until its defeat at the 2013 federal election, can be seen as a vernacular manifestation, mediated by Australian education federalism, of what Sahlberg (2011) has called GERM, the Global Education Reform Movement. This approach to school and system reform in response to globalisation has the following features: prescribed curriculum, focus on literacy and numeracy, top-down, test-based accountability, standardised teaching and learning and market-oriented reforms (e.g. management models from the private sector, school and parental choice discourses) (Sahlberg, 2011, p. 103). This reform agenda has seen the New Basics, and its approach to curriculum, move rapidly off the agenda in Queensland. In the longer term, we also think the Australian Curriculum might represent a challenge to the Queensland form of school-based, teacher-moderated assessment at the senior levels and its implicit trust of teachers and their professionalism. As already noted, the state conservative government is also reviewing this mode of assessment; as well, there has been a state parliamentary committee investigation of this mode of assessment specifically in relation to mathematics, physics and chemistry. The national reform agenda has been a component contributing to the withering of the New Basics reforms and more importantly its philosophy. What we have is a new policy focus and some policy borrowing from other national settings (Lingard, 2010) with Australian developments framed by globalizsd education policy discourses (Rizvi & Lingard, 2010), particularly in respect of knowledge and skills relevant to Organisation for Economic Cooperation and Development (OECD) testing regimes.

On the first NAPLAN in 2008, Queensland students performed badly, especially when compared with those in New South Wales and Victoria. In response to huge media coverage and political pressure, the Premier Anna Bligh (previously education minister) appointed the head of the Australian Council for Educational Research (ACER), Professor Geoff Masters to report on changes in Queensland schooling, as a way to enhance Queensland's comparative performance on NAPLAN. Interestingly, Queensland's apparently declining performance on the International Association for the Evaluation of Educational Achievement's (IEAs) Trends in International Maths and Science Study (TIMSS) was also a factor in the appointment of the Review (see Masters, 2009).

One specific policy outcome of the *Masters Report* was the implementation of Teaching and Learning Audits in all Queensland government schools, a manifestation of the 'audit cultures' accompanying state restructures (Power, 1997). Consequently, much more time was also spent in schools preparing students for the tests. This was the major interim recommendation of the Review. The publication of NAPLAN results on the *My School* website, created by the federal government in 2010 as part of its accountability and transparency agenda, has strengthened this teaching to the test, as has extensive media coverage of school and system performance with the publication of school league tables of performance. While Queensland's 2009–2012 performances were better than that of 2008, all other states had improved as well, perhaps suggesting much more time spent on preparing students for NAPLAN in all Australian schools.

The rise and fall of the New Basics in Queensland

In 1998, in the final chapter of the Conservative Queensland Borbidge government (1996–1998)[1] the *Leading Schools* initiative had been launched. While this was largely an experiment in school-based management, it also sought to improve student outcomes through the adoption of educational concepts developed in the USA by Newmann and Associates (1996) from the University of Wisconsin–Madison's Centre on Organization and Restructuring of Schools. Because of their focus upon student engagement and higher order thinking, Newmann and Associates' 'authentic' pedagogies and 'authentic' assessment promised better student outcomes in both learning and equity. This research became the construct, albeit reconceptualised and recontextualised, upon which the QSRLS began to evaluate Queensland's *Leading Schools*' initiative.[2]

The election of Labor leader, Peter Beattie, as State Premier in 1998 saw him launch his 'Smart State' strategy in which he identified knowledge, creativity and innovation as drivers of economic growth (see Adie, 2008). This was followed by extensive community consultation for developing long-term goals for schooling that would underpin the *Queensland State Education – 2010* (QSE – 2010) initiative. The *QSE – 2010* consultation process sought to investigate the major challenges facing Education Queensland such as student retention rates, the drift of students to the private sector, as well as the implications for education of broader economic and social changes related to globalisation and the growth of the knowledge economy. In the course of this process, many stakeholders questioned the extent to which Queensland education was preparing young people for a globalised, technologically driven future.

Such concerns were confirmed in the findings of the QSRLS, which had continued under the Beattie government with the support of senior policy-makers and the Minister, then Anna Bligh. The QSRLS was conducted over a period of 3 years and extended upon the work of Newmann and Associates' conceptual framework of 'authentic' pedagogies and 'authentic' assessment, with a focus on social as well as academic outcomes form schooling. The QSRLS models of 'productive' pedagogies and 'productive' assessment provided the lenses needed to evaluate pedagogies in Queensland classrooms.

The QSRLS mapped the pedagogies and assessment practices of approximately 250 teachers in four lessons each, across 24 primary and secondary schools over 3 years. Classroom observations and samples of student work were scaled via 20 pedagogic items and 18 assessment items in order to code the work of teachers and the outcomes of their students. Subsequently, these items were grouped into four domains of productive pedagogies: intellectual quality; connectedness; supportive classroom environment; and working with and valuing difference. The additional emphasis upon the social outcomes form schooling, namely, inclusivity, active citizenship and group identities, differentiated the Queensland study from that of Newmann and Associates. While rating Queensland teachers' pedagogies highly on the dimension of care and supportiveness, the findings of the QSRLS showed low and concerning levels of intellectual demand, connectedness and recognition of difference in classroom practices. Assessment tasks also rated poorly with not enough intellectual demand and with teachers seemingly not recognising the need to align assessment and pedagogy with curriculum purposes.

Responding to these findings was fundamental to achieving the *QSE – 2010* strategic priorities that promised a future-oriented curriculum for the New Millennium. The 'Framework Project' was the first step towards formulating a planned response (Education Queensland, 2004a) and this initiative subsequently delivered the New Basics Project. Drawing upon the QSRLS report, the four domains of productive pedagogies and productive assessment became one key contributor to the *Smart State* initiative and a fundamental element of the New Basics reform.

However, a parallel quasi-national curriculum reform had been in place across Australian states and territories during the 1990s, led by federal Labor governments (1983–1996). This was the organisation of school curricula into eight KLAs based upon related fields of knowledge. For example, Studies of Society and the Environment (SOSE) comprised knowledge and skills from the disciplinary fields of history, geography and economics. SOSE also included related elements of culture, values and citizenship. In contrast and more radically, the New Basics Project erased the 'subject' map' in favour of starting with 'real world' tasks, later known as 'Rich Tasks' and goals about future workers and citizens. Teachers had to begin with 'the problem' and 'backward map' to determine what skills and knowledge (repertoires of practices) would be required by students in order to solve it. According to the *New Basics Report*, 'the New Basics program is based on ... envisioning the kinds of life worlds and human subjects that the education system wants to contribute to and build' (Education Queensland, 2004a, p. 3). Here we see a new rationale for school curriculum, one not based in behavioural objectives, not based on disciplines, but rather framed through a visioning of future workers, citizens and a desired future world. For teachers, these ideas were revolutionary and a comprehensive trial was needed to evaluate their worth. This trial occurred between 2000 and 2003, involving 38 state government primary and secondary schools across Queensland.

Appropriating the political rhetoric of the Right, 'the basics' soon became 'the *New* Basics' as Professor Luke, along with the QSRLS team, began redefining the fundamental knowledge, skills and attributes needed in a globalising world of new economies, new workplaces, new technologies, diverse communities, complex cultures and new citizenship of the 'New Times' (Hall, 1996) of the approaching New Millennium. This was the context within which Queensland's New Basics Project was launched. Its rationale was that the global citizen of the New Millennium required an education that provided more than the 'old basics' of 'reading, writing and arithmetic'. The *New* 'basics' would facilitate knowledge and skills that would respond to the conditions of Hall's 'New Times': 'new economies, new workplaces, new technologies, new student identities, diverse communities, and complex cultures' (Education Queensland, 2004a, p. 2). Also fundamental to the New Basics Project was the explicit attempt to improve student outcomes and close the disadvantage gaps among diverse groups of students by uniquely aligning the three message systems of curriculum, pedagogy and assessment. We note that the name 'New Basics' flowed from market research that showed this nomenclature appealed to both conservatives and progressives in the broader community.

At the heart of the New Basics was the premise that educational reform would not eventuate if changes were made to curriculum or pedagogy or assessment practices in isolation from each other. First, it was necessary to 'unclutter' the crowded curriculum via four curriculum 'organisers': life pathways and social futures; multiliteracies and communication media; active citizenship; and environments and technologies. Students would engage with 'core tasks' (rich tasks) – real-world problems that, in their 'unpacking', would facilitate the acquisition of the knowledge and skills needed for New Times. This attempt at uncluttering was driven by a desire to enhance the depth of knowledge dealt with in classrooms. However, for Luke and his team, such reshaping of the curriculum was just the beginning, stating that 'it won't make a difference if our pedagogy isn't up to scratch' (Luke, 1999, p. 4). Thus, the third element of the New Basics triad (complementing its curriculum and pedagogy) was an approach to assessment that drew upon the work of Vygotsky's (1978) constructivism, Newman and Associates' (1996) authentic assessment, Freire's conscientisation and Dewey's (2001) project learning, to propose student-centred, constructivist, complex assessment tasks – 'Rich Tasks' – for demonstrating learning outcomes that would then be collaboratively graded and moderated by teachers. This would see the migration of teacher moderation practices, central to senior schooling in Queensland, to primary and lower secondary levels.

These rich tasks were divided into three suites: Years 1–3, 4–6 and 7–9. They included such activities as multimedia presentations, creation of student web pages, artistic performances, and designing structures for the built environment, to name but three examples of the challenging tasks (Education Queensland, 2004b) that would facilitate the education of young people for a global New Times. The tasks also required public presentations to other classes in the school and to community pace Dewey's concept of a project. The New Basics also aimed to address the needs of the most 'at risk' students in the classroom.

Unfortunately, at the present moment, Australian educational authorities are still struggling to address much the same issues, including the intransigent social class/race/gender performance nexus. Despite incremental progress over the last few years, for indigenous students, school completion rates remain at 52.9% for girls and 49.2% for boys (Australian Bureau of Statistics, 2012). Progress has also been slow for other groups of disadvantaged young people. Between 2006 and 2011, Year 12 completion (or equivalent) for young people from the *lowest* socio-economic status (SES) backgrounds rose from 71.6% to 73.7%; however, significant gaps are evident when this is compared to a national completion rate of 85% and 93.3% for young people from the *highest* SES backgrounds (Council of Australian Governments, 2013). School refusal, student disengagement and perceptions of falling academic standards continue to preoccupy educational bureaucrats and politicians, as well as remaining key foci in the research interests of education academics (see Mills & McGregor, 2014). National political panic also continues in relation to Australia's declining position on international testing such as the OECD's Programme for International Student Assessment (PISA) (Sellar & Lingard, 2013).

While the New Basics experiment indicated that its tenets had the potential to deliver intellectually in the classroom, it struggled to surmount systemic obstacles: staffing and resourcing, change weariness and, in some cases, teachers' lack of pedagogical content knowledge. The latter, perhaps paradoxically, demonstrated the necessity of deep disciplinary knowledge for teachers for successful implementation of the New Basics. The election of the Rudd federal Labor government in late 2007 strengthened the national presence in schooling in Australia, signalling the end of ambitiously experimental educational projects. As a new progressivist response to the New Times of a globalising world, the New Basics was discarded. Queensland's poor performance on the 2008 NAPLAN was central to the adoption by the State of a focus on improving test results, as was the State's response to pressures on performance stemming from national accountability and funding (Lingard & Sellar, 2013).

The national schooling agenda: the Australian curriculum and NAPLAN

Post 2007, a new national approach to education in Australia comprised national accountabilities and testing, a national curriculum and a range of National Partnerships between the federal government and the states and territories. The Australian Curriculum, Assessment and Reporting Authority (ACARA) oversees the national curriculum and testing and accountability. Another significant national development has been the creation of ACARA's *My School* website, which lists a school's results on NAPLAN against national averages and also the school's performance measured against 60 'statistically similar schools' across the nation on a socio-economic scale (Index of Community Socio-Educational Advantage – ICSEA) developed by ACARA. In the early stages of Rudd's prime ministership, these developments were facilitated by a new cooperative federalism in respect of schooling, facilitated by the reality of Labor governments in all the states and territories. This situation has now changed. However, as noted already, this changed political situation has not weakened the national agenda in schooling; indeed, there seems to be bipartisan support for a national approach to schooling in the context of globalisation from the recently elected federal Liberal National government.

The impetus towards the formulation of a national curriculum in Australia had its naissance in the 1980s when the then Federal Minister for Education, Training and Employment, John Dawkins, initiated the first moves with the states to begin outlining a common national curriculum (Dawkins, 1988). While this initiative produced agreement on the eight KLAs, state and federal political animosities and rivalries hindered any real progress until the Melbourne Declaration of 2008, which finally produced an agreement for the development of a national curriculum, initially in 'core' subjects of English, science and mathematics, but also in history due to the so-called 'history wars' between conservative politicians and historians and their more leftist counterparts as they struggled for control over the national narrative.

The Australian Curriculum has been founded upon the Melbourne Declaration and its 'Goals for Young Australians' agreed to by all systems in Australia: (1) Australian schooling promotes equity and excellence; and (2) all young Australians become successful learners, confident and creative individuals, and active and informed citizens. A closer examination of these goals reveals that the first goal has a focus on providing educational access, equity and social justice in respect of knowledge and skills; the second goal, on the other hand, echoes a common educational response to the needs of a globalised economy: developing personal qualities and dispositions best suited to globally oriented twenty-first-century societies. Indeed, the preamble to the Melbourne Declaration exhibits a very strong concern for preparing students for a global world, making four explicit statements about its significance:

(1) In the twenty-first century, Australia's capacity to provide a high quality of life for all will depends on the ability to compete in the global economy on knowledge and innovation.
(2) Global integration and international mobility have increased rapidly in the past decade.
(3) Globalisation and technological change are placing greater demands on education and skill development in Australia and the nature of jobs available to young Australians is changing faster than ever.
(4) Australia has developed a high-quality, world-class schooling system, which performs strongly against other countries of the OECD (Melbourne Declaration, 2008).[3]

Thus, the foundations of the Australian Curriculum reflect a global orientation, alongside a return to disciplinary knowledge, as evidenced in notions of educational 'excellence' and strengthening the competitive edge with like nations. This is a vernacular expression of a globalised education policy discourse.

There are early signs that the new Abbott conservative government is keen to reshape the Australian Curriculum; the Australian History Curriculum has been criticised by the new Education Minister, Christopher Pyne, as being underpinned by left-wing ideologies (Hurst, 2013). While there is commitment to a discipline-based curriculum, there is debate over the selection of knowledge in the national history curriculum. In the same interview, Pyne went on to say, 'my instincts tell me that a back-to-basics approach to education is what the country is looking for, what parents feel comfortable about' (Hurst, 2013). He also criticised child-centred and project-based learning in favour of 'direct instruction' in 'the facts'. As we write this paper, it is still unclear what this will mean for the future of the Australian Curriculum. From a Bernsteinian (1971) perspective, it would seem to foreshadow a return to 'strong classification', whereby subject disciplines are rigidly circumscribed; and 'strong framing', which vests most power in the hands of curriculum writers to determine what knowledge 'counts' in the classroom. A return to such traditional structures would potentially entrench middle-class educational advantage particularly, when coupled with the current regimes of testing and accountability.

Given that each state had shaped its own, very different, education system since before Federation, it was never going to be an easy task to reach consensus on a national curriculum. Subject writing and advisory teams were formed in 2008 and 4 years later, in 2012, English, mathematics and science curricula began implementation for P-10, with history coming on board in 2013. It must be noted here that the states were given the responsibility for implementation in respect of timelines, assessment practices and support materials for teachers and schools. The Australian Curriculum provides the state curriculum authorities the required framework in each subject (and more are in the pipeline) for what to teach, along with a set of achievement standards for each year level.

The *My School* website created by the federal Labor government in 2010 as part of their accountability and transparency agenda and also the 'school choice' discourse has also been embraced by this conservative Abbott government. Teachers' unions continue to question the validity of the data and highlight its likely negative effects on curricula and pedagogy, the likelihood of league tables of performance and the related potential for the 'naming' and 'shaming' of poorly performing schools, often situated within lower SES communities. Additionally, despite claims to the contrary, the literacy and numeracy tests which underpin *My School* have quickly become high stakes for systems and schools (Lingard & Sellar, 2013), with all the potentially negative effects on pedagogies and curricula as evidenced in other national systems (Hursh, 2008; Stobart, 2008). It would seem that Australia is continuing to adopt policies close to GERM in respect of assessment and accountability, while simultaneously attempting to successfully implement a discipline-based national curriculum that may soon be more reflective of last-century models of school subjects, than those connected with and responsive to global needs and contexts. We note here the heavy content focus of the national curriculum.

As a coherent response to a globalising world, the Australian Curriculum is a 'work-in-progress'; indeed, as an online initiative it has been conceptualised as such and as we write, it is up to Version 5.1 for the P-10 curriculum. Constructed as a series of interconnected online documents (downloadable if you wish) makes it easier to be responsive to changes and developments in the so-called 'knowledge economy'.

Threaded across each subject area are the 'general capabilities', identified as being essential skills for 'students to live and work successfully in the twenty-first century', namely, 'literacy, numeracy, information and communication technology capability; critical and creative thinking; personal and social capability and ethical understanding and intercultural understanding'. Alongside the general capabilities, sit the 'cross-curriculum priorities' justified by the claim that 'The Australian Curriculum has been written to equip young Australians with the skills, knowledge and understanding that will enable them to engage effectively with and prosper in a globalised world' (Australian Curriculum, 2013). These three additional strands comprise Aboriginal and Torres Strait Islander histories and cultures; Asia and Australia's engagement with Asia and Sustainability. We see here an approach to curriculum based on what the system wants students to become, accompanying the discipline-based focus on what students ought to learn, located in contemporary Australian (e.g. the need for reconciliation with indigenous Australians) and global politics (e.g. global warming and the so-called Asian century).

The Australian Curriculum website is organised such that there are multiple hyperlinks to guide educators towards a vast array of elements that must be considered when developing programmes of work in schools: knowledge, skills, scope and sequence; general capabilities and cross-curriculum priorities; assessment standards and models of student work for each year level. Navigating all these requirements is the responsibility of state curriculum authorities, and schools and teachers are expected to use state sites and support materials for implementation. It is at this point of 'translation' that many teachers may get lost, particularly if, as is too often the case, they are not trained to teach particular subjects and have limited pedagogical content knowledge.

At first glance, the Australian Curriculum may appear to be content-heavy, particularly if educators do not read the fine print of the state mediating documents. For example, it is often overlooked that the Australian History Curriculum allows significant freedom for local decision-making, even in high school as evident in the following note: 'The order and detail in which the content descriptions are taught are programming decisions. The number of units planned may vary depending on local decisions about how to deliver or integrate the curriculum content' (Queensland Studies Authority, 2013a). Each subject expresses this freedom to make decisions a little differently, but in various ways it underpins the whole curriculum; for example, science recommends:

> Schools develop learning contexts to suit the content to be taught and students' interests and learning needs. It is important to actively engage students in learning that is relevant and of interest to them. The focus or context for learning should connect with issues of personal or social relevance to students. (Queensland Studies Authority, 2013b)

However, as with other curricular reforms, in Queensland in particular, authorities have decided to embrace rapid implementation which has contributed to a variety of misunderstandings about the intent of the curriculum. We argue that one of the strengths of the New Basics reform was the alignment of Bernstein's message systems of curriculum, pedagogy and assessment. In the Australian Curriculum, pedagogy is not addressed and apart from establishing some broad assessment standards, the mode and manner of assessment is the responsibility of the states. Thus, without sufficient professional development for teachers and more expert federal mediation of the Australian Curriculum, a heavy content focus is almost an inevitable outcome.

We also suggest that, for these same reasons, embedding the general capabilities and the cross-curriculum priorities may falter under the complexity of the task for many teachers. It is therefore difficult to see how the Australian Curriculum will dispense more than the content of the disciplines and deliver on the promised responses to the demands of globalisation as planned in the Melbourne Declaration. The focus on NAPLAN performance also mediates against this direction. Indeed, we think a heavy content focus with pressures from test-based accountability will lead to a situation in schools, as documented by the QSRLS, of a focus on content coverage to the detriment of intellectual demand in pedagogies.

Conclusion

We have documented two contrasting responses to the global in Australian Curriculum reforms: the New Basics trial in Queensland and the discipline-based Australian Curriculum in P-10, complemented by general capabilities and cross-curriculum priorities, with the latter having similar rationales as the New Basics. We must, of course, remember that the New Basics was only ever a trial – most Queensland schools continued with a KLA curriculum overseen by the Queensland Studies Authority. In Queensland, the P-10 Australian Curriculum in mathematics, science and English was implemented in 2012 with history in 2013. Other P-10 subjects will follow. Queensland opted early to adopt in full the Australian Curriculum compared with other states such as Western Australia, which is yet to begin the implementation of the first tranche of P-10 subjects, and New South Wales, which has embedded the national in the state curriculum.

Both the New Basics and the Australian Curriculum were/are curriculum developments set against the context of all the changes evinced when we speak of globalisation, confirming Bernstein's sociological observation that curriculum changes are signifiers of societal developments. As we have already noted, the New Basics was a genre of curriculum emerging at the time across the globe, focusing on capabilities, competencies and dispositions and what societies want students *to become*. The tensions between curricula that foreground 'doing' over curricula that emphasise 'knowing' are still being played out across the globe (see Yates & Grumet, 2011), and are evident in academic debates in respect of the relative 'values' of different kinds of knowledge and the inequality that stems from not having access to the kind of high-status, discipline-based knowledge that facilitates civic participation, economic rewards and self-efficacy and growth (see Young, 2011). We understand the distinction between powerful discipline-based knowledge, which is often confused with their function in relation to the knowledge of the powerful.

The New Basics reform was conceived at a particular policy moment in Queensland of a social democratic Labor government, the pressing need for educational reform, a confident bureaucracy and leadership in education, good relationships between educational researchers and the bureaucracy and research informing policy. This context allowed a moment of (rearticulated) progressivism in Queensland schooling, set against the pressures of globalisation and related changes. We do not pretend that the New Basics was without its challenges, particularly in respect to resourcing and educating teachers, and in relation to teachers' disciplinary and pedagogical content knowledge, but its demise followed swiftly as the trial ended. We contend that political imperatives being driven by national accountability agendas ultimately prevented the full realisation of its philosophical framework. Indeed, it was Queensland's poor comparative performance on the 2008 NAPLAN test that closed unequivocally the moment of new progressivism in Queensland schooling. Through political interventions largely in response to widespread and critical media coverage, NAPLAN quickly became high stakes in Queensland government schools (Lingard & Sellar, 2013), with all of the effects indicated in research on the topic in other national settings (Hursh, 2008; Lipman, 2004; Nicholas & Berliner, 2007). NAPLAN remains high stakes for the school system in Queensland and concerns about performance on it have taken on meta-policy status (Lingard et al., 2013).

The Australian Curriculum now being implemented in P-10 is a more traditional curriculum than the New Basics, one constructed around disciplinary knowledge. In this respect, it is attempting to do two things: reassure a local populace that schools are providing a content-rich education that includes what is considered to be nation-building knowledge about this country (a greatly contested narrative in itself) and, focus educational knowledge and skills on areas that will allow Australian students to better compete on international tests such as PISA. Here we see the interweaving of national and global influences as shapers of the content of the Australian Curriculum. The other way in which the Australian Curriculum is evincing a response to globalisation is through the inclusion of the general capabilities and the cross-curriculum priorities, which are embedded across the subject curricula. Like the New Basics reform, these elements attempt to conceptualise part of the curriculum as preparing young people for a rapidly evolving world of new work, new cultures and new technologies, in which they will need capacities and dispositions to cope with significant global changes as implied within the goals of the Melbourne Declaration: competing in the global economy; being globally connected;

coping with technological change; developing skills in response to changing job markets in Australia and helping the nation achieve an international competitive edge.

These elements of the national curriculum have the same rationale as the New Basics and focus on what the nation wants students to become, in addition to what the nation wants them to learn. While the general capabilities and cross-curriculum priorities are laudable, we fear that the complexity of their implementation in schools' work programmes, aligned with the heavy content focus of the national curriculum, may hinder their full realisation. To this point, most attention has been focused on issues relating to the content coverage of the Australian Curriculum, along with improving NAPLAN performance across the system. We argue that the heavy content coverage of the Australian Curriculum, combined with the new and to-be-expanded testing regime, will most likely ensure the situation the productive pedagogy research found in Queensland classrooms, namely, that an emphasis on width of curriculum coverage militates against intellectual demand in pedagogies and inhibits a focus on depth of knowledge.

Our analysis has highlighted some of the challenges faced by Australian Curriculum developers as they have tried to respond to educational agendas of accountability and competitiveness, while grappling with the very real need to prepare young people, in socially just ways, for a future predicated on rapid global and technological change. It is our contention that at the current moment, an Australian vernacularised version of GERM and an inadequately implemented, discipline-based Australian Curriculum have won out over other more globally responsive manifestations of curriculum as exemplified by Queensland's New Basics trial. However, we also note that for good reasons the New Basics did not challenge the discipline-based curriculum in senior schooling in Queensland. Furthermore, Australia's federal political structure at this policy moment mediates and produces a complex division of labour in Australian schooling across the three message systems with significant impact on the enactment of the Australian Curriculum and the depth of knowledge in classroom pedagogies.

Acknowledgements

The research upon which this paper is based has been developed from an Australian Research Council (ARC) funded Discovery Project (DP1094850), Schooling the nation in an age of globalization: national curriculum, accountabilities and their effects.

Notes

1 Labor was in political power in Queensland, 1989 2012, apart from a short Conservative interregnum of the Borbidge government, 1996 1998.

2 The QSRLS was commissioned during the Borbidge government to evaluate the impact of school based management (*Leading Schools*) on equity and student learning. The election of Beattie Labor in 1998 saw this government abolish *Leading Schools*, but continue support for this research (costing $1.3 million), which evolved into a mapping of classroom practices and their effects on student learning.
3 It is interesting that Australia's apparently declining performance on PISA 2009 caused national political panic with the then Prime Minister establishing a target enschrined in legislation that Australia be back in the top five of performers by 2025, a goal supported by the new Conservative Federal Minister (see Sellar & Lingard, 2013).

References

Adie, L. (2008). The hegemonic positioning of 'Smart State' policy. *Journal of Education Policy, 23*(3), 251–264.

Australian Bureau of Statistics. (2012). *4211.0 schools*. Retrieved from http://www.abs.gov.au/AUSSTATS/abs@.nsf/Latestproducts/4221.0Main%20Features302012

Bernstein, B. (1971). On the classification and framing of educational knowledge. In M. F. D. Young (Ed.), *Knowledge and control: New directions for the sociology of education* (pp. 47–69). London: Collier-Macmillan.

Bernstein, B. (1973). *Class, codes and control, Vol. 2*. London: Routledge & Kegan Paul.

Biesta, G. (2012). Philosophy of education for the public good: Five challenges and an agenda. *Educational Philosophy and Theory, 44*(6), 581–593.

Biesta, G., & Priestley, M. (2013). Capacities and the curriculum. In M. Priestley & G. Biesta (Eds.), *Reinventing the curriculum* (pp. 35–49). London: Bloomsbury.

Council of Australian Governments. (2013). *Key findings: Education in Australia 2012: Five years of performance*. Retrieved from http://www.coagreformcouncil.gov.au/reports/education/education-australia-2012-five-years-performance

Dawkins, J. (1988). *Strengthening Australia's schools*. Canberra: Ministry for Employment, Education and Training.

Dewey, J. (2001). *The school and society; & the child and the curriculum*. Minola, NY: Dover.

Education Queensland. (2004a). *The new basics research report*. Brisbane: Department of Education.

Education Queensland. (2004b). *New basics: Rich tasks*. Brisbane: Department of Education.

Gee, J. (1999). New people in new worlds: Networks, the new capitalism and schools. In B. Kalantzis (Ed.), *Multiliteracies: Literacy, learning and the design of social futures* (pp. 43–68). London: Routledge.

Grattan, M. (2006, January 26). Howard claims victory in national culture wars. *The Age*. Retrieved from http://www.theage.com.au/news/national/pm-claims-victory-in-culture-wars/2006/01/25/1138066861163.html

Hall, S. (1996) The meaning of new times. In D. Morley & K.-H. Chen (Eds.), *Stuart hall: Critical dialogues in cultural studies* (pp. 223–237). London: Routledge.

Hayes, D., Mills, M., Christie, P., & Lingard, B. (2006). *Teachers and schooling making a difference*. Sydney: Allen and Unwin.

Hursh, D. (2008). *High-stakes testing and the decline of teaching and learning*. Lanham, MD: Rowman and Littlefield.

Hurst, D. (2013, September 28). Say after the minister: Old is new again. *The Sydney Morning Herald*. Retrieved from http://www.smh.com.au/federal-politics/political-news/say-after-the-minister-old-is-new-again-20130927-2ujhn.html

Lingard, B. (2000). Federalism in schooling since the Karmel Report (1973): From modernist hope to postmodernist performativity. *The Australian Educational Researcher, 27*(2), 25 61.

Lingard, B. (2007). Pedagogies of indifference. *International Journal of Inclusive Education, 11*(3), 245 266.

Lingard, B. (2010). Policy borrowing, policy learning: Testing times in Australian schools. *Critical Studies in Education, 51*(2), 129 147.

Lingard, B., Ladwig, J., Mills, M., Bahr, N., Chant, D., Warry, M., ... Luke, A. (2001). *The Queensland school reform longitudinal study*. Brisbane: Department of Education.

Lingard, B., Martino, W., & Rezai-Rashti, G. (2013). Testing regimes, accountabilities and education policy: Commensurate global and national developments. *Journal of Education Policy, 28*(5), 539 556.

Lingard, B., & Sellar, S. (2013). 'Catalyst data': Perverse systemic effects of audit and accountability in Australian schooling. *Journal of Education Policy, 28*(5), 634 656.

Lipman, P. (2004). *High stakes education: Inequality, globalization and urban school reform*. New York: RoutledgeFalmer.

Luke, A. (1999). *Education and new times: Why equity and social justice still matter, but differently*. Brisbane: Department of Education.

Lyotard, F. (1991). *The inhuman: Reflections on time*. Palo Alto, CA: Stanford University Press.

Masters, G. N. (2009). *Improving literacy, numeracy and science learning in Queensland primary schools*. Melbourne: Australian Council for Educational Research.

McLeod, J., & Yates, L. (2006). *Making modern lives: Subjectivity, schooling and social change*. New York, NY: SUNY Press.

Melbourne Declaration on Educational Goals for Young Australians. (2008). Canberra: Ministerial council on education, employment, training and youth affairs. Retrieved from: http://www.mceecdya.edu.au/verve/ resources/national declaration on the educational goals for young australians.pdf

Mills, M., & McGregor, G. (2014). *Re-engaging young people in education: Learning from alternative schools*. Abingdon: Routledge.

Newmann, F., & Associates. (1996). *Authentic achievement: Restructuring schools for intellectual quality*. San Francisco, CA: Jossey-Bass.

Nicholas, S., & Berliner, D. (2007). *Collateral damage: How high-stakes testing corrupts America's schools*. Cambridge, MA: Harvard University Press.

Power, M. (1997). *The audit society: Rituals of verification*. Oxford: Oxford University Press.

Priestley, M., & Biesta, G. (Eds.). (2013). *Reinventing curriculum: New trends in curriculum policy and practice*. London: Bloomsbury.

Queensland Studies Authority. (2013a). *Prep to YYear 10: Australian Curriculum in Queensland*. Retrieved from http://www.qsa.qld.edu.au/yr8-history-curriculum.html

Queensland Studies Authority. (2013b). *The Australian Curriculum in Queensland*. Retrieved from http://www.qsa.qld.edu.au/yr8-science-curriculum.html

Rizvi, F., & Lingard, B. (2010). *Globalizing education policy*. London: Routledge.

Robbins, B. (1998). Comparative cosmopolitanisms. In P. Cheah & B. Robbins (Eds.), *Cosmoplitics* (pp. 246 264). Minneapolis, MN: University of Minnesota Press.

Sahlberg, P. (2011). *Finnish lessons: What can the world learn from educational change in Finland?* New York, NY: Teachers' College Press.

Sellar, S., & Lingard, B. (2013). 'Looking East': Shanghai, PISA 2009 and the reconstitution of reference societies in the global education policy field. *Comparative Education, 49*(4), 464–485.

Stobart, G. (2008). *Testing times: The uses and abuses of assessment.* London: Routledge.

Vygotsky, L. S. (1978). *Mind in society: The development of higher psychological processes.* Cambridge, MA: Harvard University.

Whitty, G. (2010). Revisiting school knowledge: some sociological perspectives on new school curricula. *European Journal of Education, 45*(1), 28–45.

Williams, C., Gannon, S., & Sawyer, W. (2013). A genealogy of the 'Future': Antipodean trajectories and travels of the '21st century learner'. *Journal of Education Policy, 28*(6), 792–806.

Wyse, D., Baumfield, V., Egan, D., Hayward, L., Hulme, M., Menter, I., … Lingard, B. (2012) *Creating the curriculum.* London: Routledge.

Yates, L., & Grumet, M. (Eds.). (2011). *Curriculum in today's world: Configuring knowledge, identities, work and politics.* London: Routledge.

Young, M. (2011). Curriculum policies for a knowledge society. In L. Yates & M. Grumet (Eds.), *Curriculum in today's world: Configuring knowledge, identities, work and politics.* London: Routledge.

Dysfunctional dichotomies? Deflating bipolar constructions of curriculum and pedagogy through case studies from music and history

Tim Cain[a] and Arthur Chapman[b]

[a]*Faculty of Education, Edge Hill University, Ormskirk, England;* [b]*Department of Curriculum, Pedagogy and Assessment, Institute of Education, London, England*

> Recent public discussions of curriculum and pedagogy that have accompanied the English National Curriculum review have been structured around clichéd dichotomies that generate more heat than light and that, as Robin Alexander has argued, reduce complex educational debates to oppositional and incompatible slogans. This paper begins by exploring the ways in which these dichotomies have structured recent debates and goes on to critically explore arguments in two contemporary debates, in the fields of history education and music education, assessing how these debates have been framed and the extent to which the debates can be considered fruitful and progressive. In the first case, we seek to show, through a discussion of 'knowledge' and 'skill' in history, that bipolar thinking is both inadequate and dysfunctional in relation to the matters under discussion. A third term – disciplinary understanding – is advocated and explored. In the second case, we demonstrate that dichotomous thinking about formal and informal music education has generated a debate that has become more sophisticated as various authors have problematised and critiqued informal learning. Analysis of these debates suggests that dichotomous thinking is pernicious when dichotomies are used only as slogans, although dichotomies can be generative when they are used as starting points to open discussion, not to close it. The paper suggests that the difference between the debates might be explained by the varying degrees of political involvement in them.

Introduction: dysfunctional dichotomies

Beyond dichotomous pedagogies is the title of a paper by Robin Alexander. Originally a conference paper in 2002, it was revised in 2006 and again in 2008. In it, Alexander (2008) argued against, 'the reduction of complex educational debates to bipolar slogans cast in a state of permanent and irreconcilable opposition' (p. 72). These bipolar slogans included focusing educational endeavour on the child rather than the curriculum, on learning rather than teaching and (quoting the Hadow Report of 1931) on 'activity and experience' rather than 'knowledge to be acquired and facts to be stored'. Alexander (2008) claimed that the tendency, to view educational debates in dichotomous terms, appealed to politicians and the press ('for the purposes of selling newspapers and winning elections', p. 73) but dichotomies were ultimately pernicious because they misrepresented reality and, on occasions, 'can harm the very people whose interests they claim to serve' (p. 74). The present paper examines two contemporary debates, in the fields of history education and music education. It demonstrates that dichotomous thinking is still evident but suggests that its effects are not necessarily pernicious if dichotomies are used as a starting point for debate.

History: distracting dichotomies and restricted options

Public discussions of history curriculum and pedagogy in England tend to be structured through stark dichotomies – between 'content' and 'skills' and between 'traditional' and 'progressive' and 'child-centred' and 'subject-centred' pedagogies (Lee, 2011, pp. 132–134; Phillips, 1998). These oppositions are – and have long been known to be – at best overdrawn and at worst erroneous: to be distracting dichotomies (Counsell, 2000) and 'misplaced slogans and polarities' (Lee, 2011, p. 132). They persist, nonetheless, and continue to impact and deform public discussions of history curriculum, pedagogy and assessment in England, as recent processes of curriculum reform show.

The neo-traditional critics of current educational practices who have driven curriculum reform processes in England since 2010 counter-pose 'the teaching of knowledge' to 'the skill of learning "how to learn"' (Gibb, 2012) and argue against 'a curriculum built on... diffuse abstract outcomes' and 'abstract skills' and for 'traditional, academic, fact-rich, knowledge-centred, subject-based, teacher-led education' (Gove, 2008). Discipline is valorised in this neo-traditional discourse and disciplined history education is typically presented as involving little more than the mastery of extensive information in chronological sequence (Gibb, 2012; Gove, 2009, 2013b). Discipline, understood as the acquisition and use of information, is counter-posed to skills and the latter are either dismissed (Gibb, 2012) or given a secondary and subservient role (Gove, 2013a).

These neo-traditionalist arguments are presented as grounded in 'accumulation of evidence – from schools, states and scientists' and as 'close to being irrefutable' (Gove, 2013a). To exemplify:

> It is only when knowledge is secure in the long-term memory that it can be summoned up effortlessly and the working memory can be freed to deal with new and challenging tasks... the more people know about any subject domain the easier it is for them to store and utilise new information

creatively... critical thinking skills - such as... interrogating sources in history - depend on extensive background knowledge - about what... might be suspicious omissions in a contemporary account of events. (Gove, 2013a)

In fact, as we will show, these claims are more than refutable and rest on an erroneous and two-dimensional conception of what learning history involves. Historical thinking is misunderstood if it is characterised simply in terms of the exercise of generic 'thinking skills' grounded in the mastery of 'extensive' information about the past and curriculum proposals that aim to develop historical understanding must move beyond 'skills' and 'information', as alternatives or in combination.

Beyond the information given

The narrative underlying neo-traditional critiques of current curriculum, pedagogy and assessment is bipolar and melodramatic – a narrative of betrayal in which ideologically motivated advocates of 'skills' are characterised as having progressively devalued 'knowledge' since the 1960s (Gibb, 2012; Gove, 2008, 2010).

This narrative gains some traction from the emphasis placed on 'skills' in the 'New History' emerging from the Schools Council History Project in the early 1970s: it is certainly true that many advocates of 'new' history placed great emphasis on *Skills in History*, to cite the title of a popular textbook (Shuter & Child, 1987); however, the aim of the 'new' history was to develop pupil understandings of a 'form of knowledge' (Rogers, 1979; Shemilt, 1980, 1983) rather than of 'skills' as opposed to 'knowledge' or of 'knowledge' as opposed to 'skills'. Advocacy of learning history as a form of knowledge involves a great deal more than the advocacy of generic skills. The textbook we have cited, for example, focused on 'skills and concepts... and... knowledge and understanding' (Shuter & Child, 1987) and the 'skills' advocated by the 'New History' were understood as specific to history rather than as generic and as part of wider package of history-specific knowledge and conceptual understanding (Rogers, 1979; Shemilt, 1980, 1983). In any case, for many advocates of a 'form of knowledge' approach to the history curriculum, talk of skills misses the point and learning history is a matter of developing history-specific understandings rather than generic 'skills':

> Skills are commonly single-track activities, such as riding a bicycle, which may be learned and improved through practice. The understandings at stake in history are complex and demand reflection. Students are unlikely to acquire [these] understandings by practice alone; they need to think about what they are doing and the extent to which they understand it. (Lee, 2005, pp. 40–41)

It is clear, then, that the neo-traditionalist account of the recent history of history education in England is an inaccurate one that misunderstands the 'New History'. It also misunderstands its immediate target – the 2008 National Curriculum (Qualifications and Curriculum Authority [QCA], 2007) – and pedagogic practice in contemporary history classrooms (Counsell, 2011). The former, as a cursory inspection of its curriculum architecture demonstrates, is organised around 'content', 'concepts' and 'processes' (QCA, 2007): skills play a minor role in the document.[1] The latter, as Christine Counsell has argued, has been characterised by the development, in the period since the introduction of the National Curriculum in 1991, of a sustained teacher discourse focused on 'relating disciplinary practices to meaningful activity for children' often in the face of and despite wider systemic pressures to adopt 'genericist' pedagogies (Counsell, 2011, p. 204).

Notwithstanding its irrelevance to the understanding of history education practice, the advocacy of 'generic skills' in general pedagogic discourse has been a very real element of the recent history of wider curriculum debate in England (Hills, 2004; Royal Society for the Arts, n. d., 2005): in the age of the search engine that can 'retrieve' information instantly, one influential argument suggests, what matters is information literacy (as it were, the 'skills' of mindful searching and processing) and not information itself (Mitra, 2013). There is a parallel between genericist transferrable skills arguments and neo-traditional 'core knowledge' arguments and both are the mirror image of each other. Where genericists valorise information processing (generic skills), neo-traditionalists valorise information possession (core knowledge), yet both model thinking as information processing and reduce subject disciplines to bodies of knowledge, to be valued, mastered and memorised (neo-traditionalists) or to be dismissed and simply looked-up when necessary (genericists). Both positions neglect the fact that disciplines are *forms* of knowledge, not just *bodies* of knowledge, and the fact that, as the American National Research Council have shown, more than two dimensions are necessary if we are to model and understand learning in subject disciplines:

> To develop competence in an area of inquiry, students must: (1) have a deep foundation of factual knowledge, (2) understand facts and ideas in the context of a conceptual framework and (3) organise knowledge in ways that facilitate retrieval and application (Donovan & Bransford, 2005, p. 1).

Reading informatically and reading historically

Among the key sources cited in support of neo-traditionalist claims about the priority of extensive background knowledge the work of E. D. Hirsch has particular prominence (Gibb, 2012). It is worth looking in some detail at this work to assess its implications for teaching and learning in history.

The core contention of E. D. Hirsch's *Cultural Literacy* (1988) is that possession of information is key to literacy. This claim is urged against what Hirsch calls advocates of educational 'formalism' (Rousseau, Wordsworth, Dewey) who, according to Hirsch, devalue content and advocate generic reading 'skills'. Reading comprehension research has shown, Hirsch (1988) contends, that:

> [W]e cannot treat reading and writing as empty skills, independent of specific knowledge... The level of literacy exhibited in each task depends on the relevant background information that the person possesses. (p. 8)

Literacy is modelled by Hirsch in terms of the role of long- and short-term memory in comprehension and Hirsch contends that communication in speech or writing depends, fundamentally, on the possession of large amounts of medium-complexity 'telegraphic, vague and limited' information (Hirsch, 1988, p. 26) schematised in the long-term memory in organised and 'retrievable form' (Hirsch, 1988, p. 56). If a student does not possess relevant and rapidly retrievable background information they will not be able to understand the speech or the writing of others and, for Hirsch, the information-gathering skills, celebrated by Mitra and others (Mitra, 2013), are no solution: if a student tried to compensate for information deficits by trying to retrieve and assimilate material from dictionaries and other long-term memory proxies they would become trapped in high cognitive-load activity and cognitive short circuits (Hirsch, 1988, pp. 51–54). These facts about cognitive architecture show, for Hirsch, that generic thinking processes are an educational blind alley: the generic – if it exists at all – must depend on the particular and specific (long-term memory cultural resources).

Cognitive science further shows, Hirsch contends, that generic processes do not exist in any case: thinking, for Hirsch, is always and inevitably thinking about something in the context of specific disciplines, understood as bodies of information (Hirsch, 1988, pp. 125–133), an argument Hirsch had made earlier, in work on hermeneutics, on philosophical grounds (Hirsch, 1966, p. vi):

> Aristotle's idea that each discipline has its own distinctive and autonomous method has been widely and inappropriately applied to the various disciplines of textual interpretation... The accurate form of Aristotle's conception, as applied to hermeneutics, is that each interpretive problem requires its own distinct context of relevant knowledge. (Hirsch, 1966, p. vii)

Among the evidence Hirsch adduces in support of his claim that the possession of key information is key to literacy is data from a study conducted with co-workers in the late 1970s that explored the effect of knowledge on reading rate. Respondents in two contexts (a university and a community college) were given pristine and degraded versions of texts to read and impacts of context and of text degradation on reading rates were compared. One pair of texts depended upon specific historical background knowledge about the American Civil War. Where no specialist background knowledge was presupposed, there were no differences in performance between the two groups of students, however, where knowledge was relevant the differences between the two groups were marked (Hirsch, 1988, pp. 45–47). Hirsch's inference is that it is the possession of background information (such as who Ulysses S. Grant was or where and what Appomattox was) that explains these differences.

What do studies of the reading strategies deployed by expert and novice historical thinkers tell us about the weight that we should place on Hirsh's arguments? Sam Wineburg's studies of historical reading and historical thinking (Wineburg, 2001, 2007) rely on the close collection of detailed qualitative data, using 'think aloud' protocols, about the processes that experts and novices engage in when reading historical texts. Wineburg's studies show, first, contrary to Hirsch's hermeneutic claims, that historians read in particular ways that embody epistemic beliefs and assumptions, and second, contrary to Hirsh's claims about the importance of specific information, that the possession of information alone is not what makes the difference between experts and novices. What does make the difference is knowing how to read historically, or, to say the same thing in a different way, mastery of domain specific conceptual and procedural understandings.

In Wineburg's 1991 expert–novice study, for example, eight historians and eight high-achieving high-school students were asked to read a collection of texts of various kinds about The Battle of Lexington and to rank them in terms of reliability. Some of the historians were expert in this period and others were not and had diverse specialisms (including twentieth century labour history, medieval history, Islamic history):

> Two high school students answered more of the identification questions ('What was Fort Tichonderona?', 'Who was George Grenville?', 'What were the Townshend Acts?') than one of the historians, and another historian got only one more answer than most students. (Wineburg, 2001, p. 76)

Notwithstanding differences in 'core knowledge', dramatic differences were apparent in how the historians and the high-school students read. Whereas the historians read texts for subtext as well as for literal meaning, the high-school students focused on what the texts were literally saying. Whereas the historians continually cross-referenced between the texts that they were reading, using what was said in one to inform their readings of another and to build up an overall situation model, the students did not. Whereas the historians typically deployed a 'sourcing heuristic' (Wineburg, 2001, p. 76) – reading information provided about the origins of texts 98% of the time before reading the texts – most of the time the students did not (this occurred 31% of the time). Some of the students tended to consider the text book account within the collection to be the most reliable: 'For such students the text book, not the eye witness accounts, emerged as the primary source' (Wineburg, 2001, p. 68) and whereas 'for the students, the locus of authority was in the text; for the historians, it was in the questions that they formulated about the text' (Wineburg, 2001, p. 77).

What explains the dramatic differences in the ways in which the historians and the students went about reading these texts? For Wineburg:

> The differences in each group's approach can be traced... to sweeping beliefs about historical inquiry, or what might be called an epistemology of the text. For students reading history was not a process of puzzling about authors' intentions or situating texts in a social world but of gathering information, with texts serving as bearers of information... Before students can see subtexts, they must first believe they exist. (Wineburg, 2001, p. 76)

On this account, the dichotomy between 'skills' and 'knowledge', common to both genericist and neo-traditionalist approaches to the curriculum, misses the point. Children who are rich in information, Wineburg shows, may simply read informatically and demonstrate poor historical understanding because they hold questionable epistemic beliefs. They are, one might say, historically illiterate. To help them to read historically we need to equip them with disciplinary understanding as much, if not more than, with information and where subject disciplines like history are concerned, 'core knowledge' is not an agglomeration of singular factual statements committed to the long-term memory: the core knowledge essential to reading history includes domain specific concepts and epistemic beliefs (Gardner, 2000).

To return to the quotation from our current Secretary of State for Education cited earlier, it is certainly likely to be the case that 'extensive background knowledge' is necessary if students are to be able to meaningfully 'interrogate sources'. If it is necessary, however, it is certainly not sufficient. 'Interrogating sources' in history is certainly not a generic critical thinking skill: it has conceptual dimensions (a concept of *evidence*) and a procedural element (modes of reading and interrogation) and knowing any number of facts about the historical context of an historical document will not help students interrogate that document *as evidence* unless they have some knowledge and understanding of *the concept of evidence* and some understanding of how to ask questions and of what questions to ask (Ashby, 2011). To know a discipline is to know and understand it as both a body and as form of knowledge: knowledge that has body but no form is as valueless as knowledge that has form but no body.

Music: formal and informal approaches to pedagogy

A similar dichotomy exists within the discourse of music education, around formal and informal learning. In England, its recent manifestation was ignited by a project funded by the Paul Hamlyn Foundation, entitled *Musical Futures* and in particular, by 'a new classroom pedagogy' (Green, 2008) which, drawing on concepts of informal education (e.g. Organisation for Economic Co-operation and Development, 1995) has been termed 'informal' pedagogy. *Musical Futures* disseminates this work through approximately 60 workshops per year (Musical Futures, n.d.); a quantitative evaluation found that over 1500 teachers in England had registered with the programme (Hallam, Creech, Sandford, Rinta, & Shave, 2009) and it has inspired similar initiatives in Australia (www.musicalfuturesaustralia.org) and Canada (http://musicalfuturescanada.org/), as well as special editions of *British Journal of Music Education* and *Visions of Research in Music Education*. The *Musical Futures* website explains its genesis and purpose:

> The informal learning model was developed by Professor Lucy Green (Institute of Education University of London) and Hertfordshire Music Service. The informal learning model explores ways to enhance pupil motivation, enjoyment and skill acquisition in Key Stage 3 (i.e. 11–14 years) music lessons by tapping into the real-life learning practices of popular musicians. (Musical Futures, n.d.)

Green's 'informal learning model' is based on her ethnographical research into how garage band musicians learn to play music in informal contexts: using music they choose themselves, they learn to perform it with friends by closely listening and copying recordings – sometimes playing only a few seconds of the recordings at a time, in order to copy them accurately. In so doing, they engage in personal, often haphazard learning without structured guidance; and integrate listening, performing, improvising and composing in the learning process (Green, 2002).

Building on her (2002) findings, Green proposed a pedagogical practice in which schoolteachers ask students to use these 'informal' methods in the classroom to learn to play and sing songs. This practice was investigated in an action research project in secondary schools in England (Green, 2008). It involved a re-working of the teacher's role:

> The role of the teacher throughout the project was to establish ground rules for behaviour, set the task going at the start of each stage, then stand back and observe what pupils were doing. During this time teachers were asked to attempt to take on and empathise with pupils' perspectives and the goals that pupils set for themselves, then to begin to diagnose pupils' needs in relation to those goals. After, and only after, this period, they were to offer suggestions and act as 'musical models' so as to help pupils reach the goals

that they had set for themselves. Teachers told their pupils that they would be available for help if required, but that they would not be instructing in the normal way. (Green, 2008, pp. 24–25)

There were times when, 'there was literally no pedagogic role for teachers to play' (Green, 2008, p. 31). At other times teachers taught in a responsive way, diagnosing students' needs and making suggestions but not instructing:

> ... showing pupils how to play something but only in rough, simplified or partial form, then retreating; showing them how to hold an instrument more comfortably, but without insisting on correct hold or posture; showing them where to find notes on an instrument, but without saying exactly what to do with those notes; playing a riff or a rhythm, but without expecting accurate repetition. (p. 35)

Thus, 'teachers avoided standing over pupils to check that they were doing what they had been shown correctly, but instead left them to take the advice in their own way, or not to take it at all' (p. 35). Green (2008) found that every teacher in the action research project found the new pedagogical approach 'new, and in many cases radical and challenging' (p. 27), but they nevertheless embraced them to the extent of abandoning formal lessons, despite Green's explicit warning that, 'the project does not claim to address all possible musical skills or to be a complete curriculum' (Green, 2008, p. 24). This finding suggests that teachers were convinced by the new pedagogy and willing to change their practice, but it also suggests a lack of confidence in 'more formal' teaching which was abandoned despite recommendations to the contrary. The teachers, it seems, could not use both formal and informal approaches with the same classes; to adopt informal approaches meant abandoning formal ones.

This section reviews the literature around Green's 'informal learning model', charting the development of the debate and distinguishing strands of enthusiasm, problematisation and critique.

Enthusiasm for informal learning

One strand within the literature expresses enthusiasm for informal learning, often on ideological grounds. Although Folkestad (2006) states, 'I strongly question the sometimes implicitly normative value judgements. .. where informal is equal to good, true or authentic, while formal is equal to artificial, boring and bad' (p. 143), informal learning is seen as 'ideal' (Jenkins, 2011), 'liberatory' (Wright, 2008), 'real' (Sexton, 2012) and 'authentic' (Jaffurs, 2006). Jaffurs (2004) is a teacher's self-study, describing her conversion from a formal pedagogy ('I was totally in charge of everything they heard when they stepped across the doorway into "my" music room', p. 190) to an informal one. She describes informal learning as, 'natural and spontaneous responses to music' (p. 192) and explains how, inspired by Green's (2002) research, she studied a student rock band to discover how these students acquired, understood and valued the music they played. A crucial aspect of her conversion was the alienating experience of being an 'outsider' in the students' informal learning environment:

> As an ethnographer conducting my research, I walked down the basement stairs to observe the garage band and felt like an outsider. I realized that some of my students may feel the same way [i.e. alienated in her classroom]. (p. 198)

Convinced by her students' passion for 'their' music and their ability to learn to play it without teacher assistance, she adopted an informal approach to her teaching, listening to her students and responding to their musical preferences and passions. She concludes, 'My garage band musicians taught me not to ask my students to compose an ABA composition when they want to write a rap' (p. 199).

On a more theoretical level, Wright (2008) relates Green's (2008) informal model to Freire's (1970) concept of liberatory education. Associating formal education with Freire's 'banking' model, she finds parallels between Freire's vision of empowering students by being given control over their own learning, which starts in the learner's everyday, lived experience, and Green's informal pedagogy. Similarly, from the premise that 'a good music education should bring about a fundamental change in the students' self-identity' (p. 193), Jenkins (2011) writes

> ... informal learning is not only a good way to learn, it is the ideal way to learn. .. While formal learning strategies supply much needed information and guidance, it is informal techniques that tend to compel students to make ongoing decisions in constructing simulations of real-life contexts. (Jenkins, 2011, pp. 194–195)

A related strand of the literature examines examples of informal learning in genres other than garage bands. Söderman and Folkestad (2004), investigating the learning of hip-hop musicians, explain how musicians use loops and samples of other people's music, relating this practice to Barthes' claim that a text is 'a new mixture of already existing texts' (p. 315). Importantly, they argue, the aesthetic standards of the music are set by the participants rather than a teacher. The notion of a self-determined aesthetic standard is developed in Cope's (2002) study of folk musicians. This report contrasts formal music teaching which, 'aims to develop a concert player in the Western Classical tradition', with informal learning, which generates the 'competent amateur' with 'the tune as the medium of instruction. .. there is more flexibility about some aspects of technique' (p. 94).

Cope (2002) shows that informal learning in 'sessions' provides both the motivation to learn and the means of learning. He concludes that social contexts encourage learning, whereas decontextualised (formal) learning can result in students abandoning playing and argues that, although students might not gain high levels of competence by informal learning, competence is a social construct so, 'comparisons across different cultural norms are not straightforward' (p. 102). Cope (2002) argues that the formal/informal distinction is related to musical styles: formal teaching is associated with the Western Classical tradition, learned through notated music, whereas informal learning is associated with popular styles, which are largely learnt 'by ear'.

Problematising the formal–informal dichotomy

In contrast to the largely uncritical enthusiasm noted above, some studies problematise the categories of formal and informal in music education. Folkestad (2006) distinguishes formal and informal learning in terms of its venue (e.g. school or garage), learning style (e.g. using notation or learning by ear) and intentionality: in formal situations the student consciously intends to learn (e.g. new playing techniques); in informal situations, learning occurs as a by-product of participating in music-making. He states, 'Formal/informal should not be regarded as a dichotomy, but rather as the two poles of a continuum; in most learning situations, both these aspects of learning are in various degrees present and interacting' (p. 135). Espeland (2010) endorses Folkestad's notion of a continuum and problematises the categories of venue and ownership, suggesting that teaching oneself to play music at home (i.e. 'informally') according to a published, sequenced ('formal') educational resource, can be difficult to place within formal or informal categories. Jenkins (2011) conceptualises formal learning as 'the attempt to refine, regulate and control certain aspects of informal learning', in the interests of efficiency (p. 182). He also endorses Folkestad's notion of a 'continuum' and states, 'Mixed informal and formal learning, falling in the middle of this range ... occurs in most school contexts' (p. 184).

Allsup (2003) contrasts musical learning in school (fostering individuals' cognition of abstracted and generalised knowledge) with learning out of school (involving shared cognition, contextualised reasoning and the development of situation-specific skills). Drawing on Freire (1970) he argues for democratic learning based on dialogue and mutual collaboration, which is more often found out of school, but which can be brought into school as 'a new hybrid' (p. 33). Responding to Green (2008), he cites Dewey who 'viewed informal learning as spirited and natural, but worried that its gains were too random, and its outcomes too narrow' (p. 6). Allsup (2008) expresses concern that students might not become 'media literate' in informal settings:

> ... a curriculum based on the copying of CD recordings apart from adult interaction is educationally naïve, especially when faced off against the sophistication of predatory capitalism. .. it seems prudent to provide formal spaces in which dialogue and critique can occur. (Allsup, 2008, p. 6)

A cautionary note is also sounded in a review of music in Swedish schools, where the music curriculum is largely informal:

> Usually, the students are relatively free to choose which songs they wish to play and with what students to play ... Students have the opportunity to make their own musical decisions, cooperate with one another and the music learning is mainly peer-directed. (Georgii-Hemming & Westvall, 2010, p. 23)

The review notes deficiencies of this informal approach: the choices that students make are from a limited number of musical genres, there is little composing and Information and Communications Technology (ICT) is rarely used; teachers explain these gaps by emphasising the social goals of their teaching. In a similar vein, Cain's (2013) case study of formal teaching found that formal pedagogies were more helpful than informal pedagogies for teaching conceptual material, knowledge about music and unfamiliar repertoire, i.e. 'knowledge of' music. He concludes that 'formal' and 'informal' are to be seen as educational means which can be evaluated only in the light of their intended aims.

Critiquing informal learning

More recently, writers have offered more direct critiques of informal learning. For Allsup, Westerlund, and Shieh (2012) Green's informal learning appears to be seen as a way of achieving authenticity in music education, through connecting classroom music with youth culture or 'the cultures of youth' (p. 460). Stating that education aims both to integrate students into existing society, with its past history and future hopes, and also towards personal actualisation through critique and creativity, they problematise authenticity. For them, authenticity is not located in 'relevance', understood in terms of students' preferences, however important these preferences are, because relevance alone cannot define what students need to know, to become 'critical authors of their present and imagined future lives' (p. 461). Neither is authenticity found in community music, which has failed to demonstrate a greater legitimacy in this regard than schooling, nor in static and potentially alienating images of youth culture, 'where youth, popular music, and blackness have become synonymous' (p. 468). Finally, authenticity is not found in the faithful replication of authentic musical practices because these practices are constantly changing and adapting. Therefore music educators should stop striving after authenticity by means such as Green's informal learning, and instead aim for greater agency for students, with self-actualisation as an aim and empowerment as a guiding principle. They ask:

> Rather than looking first at musical preferences, authentic musical practices, or ethnographic examinations of adolescent cultures and subcultures and then taking their self-evidence as models for practice, what if music researchers and teachers started with educational ideals? Ideals that are important for all growing persons, like empowerment, agency, criticality, ethical care, and self-discovery? (Allsup et al., 2012, p. 470)

A contrasting approach is taken by Philpott and Wright (2012), who use Bernstein's (1971) concepts of classification and framing to analyse classroom music. They explain Bernstein's view of the curriculum as a means of translating principles of power and control into educational knowledge. Power is understood in terms of specialisation: the higher degree of separation between categories or groups, the more power can accrue to those with specialised knowledge. In Bernstein's terms, 'classification' is the degree of separation between curriculum subjects. Where classification is strong, subjects and their discourses are distinct, specialised knowledge is achieved by the successful and there is sharply differentiated distribution of power. Weak classification means a blurring of subject boundaries and a more general educational discourse; power is more evenly distributed. Control is associated with 'framing': within curriculum subjects, strong framing means that learning is highly organised and sequenced; weak framing means a loose organisation of subject matter. Philpott and Wright (2012) posit three contrasting scenarios, one of which is based on Green's informal learning model, and suggest that, in Bernstein's terms, the informal learning scenario is weakly classified and weakly framed and, 'the predominant "flow" of classroom relationships is from pupil to teacher' (p. 448). However, they suggest that, when teachers provide classroom resources such as microphones, electric guitars and drum kits, these resources serve to classify the curriculum in the direction of rock and pop music, and they outline an alternative scenario which would render classroom music more democratic by virtue of being more weakly classified and framed.

This use of Bernstein's theory is illuminating and can be extended, to reveal some of what is obscured by the formal–informal dichotomy. Although Green (2008) emphasised the way in which, in her model, the activities of performing, composing and listening to music are integrated, demonstrating weak classification internally (i.e. within the subject discipline), nevertheless, focusing the curriculum on audio recordings has the effect of strongly classifying the curriculum with regard to the rest of the curriculum. This is because the content of the lessons is determined by the audio recordings and what Green (1990) had previously referred to as the music's 'inherent' meanings; music is seen as musical practice, the skills of (re)producing sound. A less strongly classified view would see music as not only practice but also a means by which people understand their lives and their world, constructing and sharing cultural meanings which are allied to social, historical and geographical contexts – what Green (1990) refers to as music's 'delineated' meanings. When the music curriculum is devoted entirely to Green's informal model, students might not encounter delineated meanings, and musical discussion among them can be limited to the accuracy of the imitation, rather than the historical or cultural meaning of the music, its lyrics and its associations with dress, venues and lifestyles – in short, the matters which make the music meaningful in its cultural context. This is important because, as Allsup (2008) says, songs can express racism, sexism and hatred, music is used for political ends, and the commercial interests of the music industries can engage teenage taste in particular, narrow and self-serving ways.

The use of Bernstein (1971) also alerts us to the notion that 'the elephant in the room' in the formal–informal discussion – the matter not discussed in the literature – is social class. Although classical and popular music might both claim wide social bases nowadays, their roots are in the contrasting worlds of church, concert halls and aristocracy on the one hand, and the home, public house and working people on the other (see, for example, Legg, 2012). For a teacher to change from formal to informal is not only about teaching role or technique; it implies a change from a focus on notated music, associated with a social elite, taught by suitably qualified tutors, to the aural transmission of music of the working classes (Cope, 2002). In music, as in other subjects, messages about power and control inhere in the choice of content, as well as in degrees of classification and framing.

Beyond dichotomies

Starting from the proposal that dichotomies misrepresent the complex reality of education and on occasions, can even be harmful, we have shown that they persist in contemporary debate. Attempts to undermine them (Alexander, 2008) have not yet succeeded.

At this juncture, one of the anonymous reviewers of this paper suggested, we might helpfully compare our cases. The reviewer noted, for example, that the 'history' case focused on teaching and the 'music' case on learning. In subsequent discussions, we found ourselves noting other differences: the 'history' case is concerned mostly with curriculum and occurs in the policy domain, the 'music' case is concerned with pedagogy and occurs at the level of practice. Ironically, we found ourselves sliding, time and again, into a mode of discussion which was itself framed around dichotomous concepts. Our discussion failed to note that each concept presumes the other and that, although logically separable, they are mutually constitutive: teaching (or curriculum or policy) shapes learning (or pedagogy or practice) and vice versa. There is, in William Carlos Williams' phrase 'an interpenetration, both ways' (Williams, 1995, p. 4).

Avoiding dichotomous thinking is therefore difficult. Words reify. To talk of 'teaching' and 'learning' is to create the illusion that these are separate 'things'. It obscures the extent to which they are mutually constitutive and mutually dependent. Yet to express ourselves efficiently for the purpose of meaningful discussion, we cannot act differently; we cannot always say 'teaching, by which I mean acting so as to bring about learning'. Dichotomies are thus inscribed into our language by virtue of the fact that we use separate terms to describe phenomena which are actually interrelated. Further, it is not always desirable to avoid dichotomies. Indeed, it is sometimes necessary to assert a position in contradistinction to another, for example, to defend State education against those who would attack it or to oppose corporal punishment in the face of those who would restore it. Not all issues can be tackled with a carefully nuanced, evenly balanced stance that respects every shade of opinion. Therefore, although dichotomies can invite adversarial and inflexible thinking that sees only stark alternatives, they are probably unavoidable and sometimes, desirable.

This paper has focused on two areas of educational debate where dichotomies have been dominant. In the history example, the 'skills'/ 'knowledge' dichotomy continues to structure public debate, despite repeated attempts to deflate it and despite the fact that it is recognised as an unhelpful distraction in academic discussions (Counsell, 2000; Lee, 2011) and the outcomes have been distinctly unhelpful and probably harmful. The curriculum that has emerged from the dichotomous clamour of 2010–2013, the product of a highly politicised and largely opaque and unaccountable process (Boffey, 2013; Cannadine, 2013; Evans, 2013; Mandler, 2013), is a weaker document than the one it replaces: whereas, as we have seen, the 2007 document's curriculum architecture explicitly modelled history in a three-dimensional and non-dichotomous way (QCA, 2007) the 2013 document's curriculum architecture is two-dimensional and divides what pupils are to learn between 'aims' and 'content'; whereas all four iterations of the curriculum since 1991 have explicitly recognised the importance of conceptual progression to historical learning (Arthur & Phillips, 2000; Davies, 2011) the 2013 document dispenses with the notion of progression and of modelling progression entirely (Department for Education [DfE], 2013). What is foregrounded in one document is in danger of vanishing in the other and, given the internationally acknowledged importance of conceptual dimensions of historical learning to pupils' ability to learn history, the outcomes for both teachers' teaching and pupils' learning seem likely to be detrimental (Bransford, Brown, & Cocking, 2000; Donovan & Bransford, 2005; Lévesque, 2008; Levstick, 2011; Van Drie & Van Boxtell, 2008).[2]

In the music example, we can see positive movement: the debate starts with dichotomous concepts but moves towards more nuanced discussion, helped by empirical evidence and insights from theory, together with contributions from people with varying experience, expertise and values. Debate also reveals what is obscured by the formal/informal dichotomy. This case suggests that debates can be advanced when dichotomies are used to open discussion, not to close it.

One problem, of course, lies not only in advancing debate but also in convincing politicians, practitioners and the communications media of the merits of more sophisticated arguments. This is difficult because, as Alexander (2008) recognised, adversarial thinking is helpful for selling newspapers and mobilising political support. It is perhaps no coincidence that the history example, which appears mired in dichotomous clamour, is also the more politically heated. In such a situation, perhaps it is the unending responsibility of the academy, constantly and patiently to test dichotomous concepts in the light of evidence and theory (more mutually constitutive dichotomies!) welcoming different people and alternative viewpoints and continually insisting: educational issues are rarely simple.

Acknowledgements

We would like to thank Dr Katharine Burn and the anonymous *Curriculum Journal* reviewers. Each provided a thorough, challenging and thought-provoking critique of an earlier version of the paper, for which we are very grateful.

Notes

1. 'Skill/s' figures 4 times in the document and 'knowledge' 12 times and a range of other terms, that go beyond the 'skill'/'knowledge' binary, have an equivalent or greater incidence: 'understanding', for example, figures 28 times (Qualifications and Curriculum Authority, 2007).
2. The 2013 document's 'Aims' section includes reference to 'concepts' and 'methods', however, as their subsumption under 'Aims' indicates, they now have a subordinate status: matters that merited three pages in 2007 (pp. 12–15) now merit seven lines (Department for Education, 2013, p. 1). The references to assessment in 2013 are minimal (representing one sentence of a five page document) and internally incoherent: reference is made to the terminal assessment of 'the matters, skills and processes specified in the programme of study' yet no 'skills' are referred to eslewhere in the document and the only other occurrence of 'process' refers to the process of historical change itself – hardly something that students can be expected to master in a school subject (DfE, 2013, p. 1).

References

Alexander, R. (2008). *Essays on pedagogy*. London and New York: Routledge.

Allsup, R. E. (2003). Mutual learning and democratic action in instrumental music education. *Journal of Research in Music Education, 51*(1), 45 68.

Allsup, R. E. (2008). Creating an educational framework for popular music in public schools: Anticipating the second-wave. *Visions of Research in Music Education, 12*, 1 12.

Allsup, R. E., Westerlund, H., & Shieh, E. (2012). Youth culture and secondary education. In G. E. McPherson & G. F. Welch (Eds.), *The Oxford handbook of music education, Volume 1* (pp. 460 475). New York, NY: Oxford University Press.

Arthur, J., & Phillips, R. (Eds.). (2000). *Issues in history teaching*. London: Routledge.

Ashby, R. (2011). Understanding historical evidence: Teaching and learning challenges. In I. Davies (Ed.), *Debates in history teaching* (pp. 137 147). London: Routledge.

Bernstein, B. (1971). On the classification and framing of educational knowledge. In M. F. Young (Ed.), *Knowledge and control: New directions for the sociology of education* (pp. 47 69). New York, NY: Collier Macmillan.

Boffey, D. (2013, February 16). 'Old school and old-fashioned': Historians turn their fire on Gove. *The Observer*. Retrieved from http://www.theguardian.com/politics/2013/feb/16/historians-gove-curriculum

Bransford, J. D., Brown, A. L., & Cocking, R. R. (Eds.). (2000). *How people learn: Brain, mind, experience and school*. Washington, DC: National Academies Press.

Cain, T. (2013). 'Passing it on': Beyond formal or informal pedagogies. *Music Education Research, 15*(1), 74 91.

Cannadine, D. (2013, March 13). The future of history. *The Times Literary Supplement*. Retrieved from http://www.the-tls.co.uk/tls/public/article1228938.ece

Cope, P. (2002). Informal learning of musical instruments: The importance of social context. *Music Education Research, 4*(1), 93 104.

Counsell, C. (2000). Historical knowledge and historical skills: A distracting dichotomy. In J. Arthur & R. Phillips (Eds.), *Issues in history teaching* (pp. 54 71). London: Routledge.

Counsell, C. (2011). Disciplinary knowledge for all, the secondary history curriculum and history teachers' achievement, *Curriculum Journal, 22*(2), 201 225.

Davies, I. (Ed.). (2011). *Debates in history teaching*. London: Routledge.

Department for Education. (2013). History programmes of study key stage 3. London: Author. Retrieved from http://www.gov.uk/government/organisations/department-for-education/series/national-curriculum

Donovan, M. S., & Bransford, J. D. (Eds.). (2005). *How students learn: History, mathematics, and science in the classroom*. Washington, DC: National Academies Press.

Espeland, M. (2010). Dichotomies in music education: Real or unreal? *Music Education Research, 12*(2), 129 139.

Evans, R. J. (2013, March 21). Michael Gove's history curriculum is a pub quiz not an education. *The New Statesman*. Retrieved from http://www.newstatesman.com/culture/culture/2013/03/michael-gove%E2%80%99s-history-curriculum-pub-quiz-not-education

Folkestad, G. (2006). Formal and informal learning situations or practices vs formal and informal ways of learning. *British Journal of Music Education, 23*(2), 135 145.

Freire, P. (1970). *Pedagogy of the oppressed.* London: Penguin.

Gardner, H. (2000). *The disciplined mind.* New York, NY: Penguin America.

Georgii-Hemming, E., & Westvall, M. (2010). Music education a personal matter? Examining the current discourses of music education in Sweden. *British Journal of Music Education, 27*(1), 21 33.

Gibb, N. (2012, October 22). Soon history will come alive again in class. *The Daily Telegraph.* Retrieved from http://www.telegraph.co.uk/education/9624840/Soon-history-will-come-alive-again-in-class.html

Gove, M. (2008). *We will reverse Labour's devaluation of exams*Speech (Speech). Retrieved from http://www.conservatives.com/News/Speeches/2008/11/Michael Gove We will reverse Labours devaluation of exams.aspx

Gove, M. (2009). *What is education for?* (Speech to the RSA). Retrieved from http://www.thersa.org/ data/assets/pdf file/0009/213021/Gove-speech-to-RSA.pdf

Gove, M. (2010). *All pupils will learn our island story* (Speech). Retrieved from http://www.conservatives.com/News/Speeches/2010/10/Michael Gove All pupils will learn our island story.aspx

Gove, M. (2013a). *The progressive betrayal* (Speech to the Social Market Foundation). Retrieved from http://www.smf.co.uk/media/news/michael-gove-speaks-smf/

Gove, M. (2013b). *What does it mean to be an educated person?* (Speech given at Brighton College). Retrieved from http://politics.co.uk/comment-analysis/2013/05/09/michael-gove-s-anti-mr-men-speech-in-full

Green, L. (1990). *Music on deaf ears: Musical meaning, ideology, education.* Manchester: Manchester University Press.

Green, L. (2002). *How popular musicians learn: A way ahead for music education.* Aldershot: Ashgate.

Green, L. (2008). *Music, informal learning and school.* Aldershot: Ashgate.

Hallam, S., Creech, A., Sandford, C., Rinta, T., & Shave, K. (2009). *Survey of Musical Futures: A report from Institute of Education, University of London for the Paul Hamlyn Foundation.* Retrieved from http://www.musicalfutures.org/resource/27229/title/instituteofeducationreportintothetakeupandimpactofmusicalfutures

Hills, G. (2004). In from the cold: The rise of vocational education. *RSA Journal,* (November), 22 25.

Hirsch, E. D. (1966). *Validity in interpretation.* New Haven and London: Yale University Press.

Hirsch, E. D. (1988). *Cultural literacy: What every American needs to know.* New York, NY: Vintage.

Jaffurs, S. E. (2004). The impact of informal music learning practices in the classroom, or how I learned how to teach from a garage band. *International Journal of Music Education, 22*(3) 189 200.

Jaffurs S. E. (2006). The intersection of informal and formal music learning practices. *International Journal of Community Music, 4*(3) 1 29. Retrieved from http://www.intellectbooks.co.uk/MediaManager/Archive/IJCM/Volume%20D/04%20Jaffurs.pdf

Jenkins, P. (2011). Formal and informal music educational practices. *Philosophy of Music Education Review, 19*(2), 179 197.

Lee, P. J. (2005). Putting principles into practice: Understanding history. In M. S. Donovan & J. D. Bransford (Eds.), *How students learn: History in the classroom* (pp. 31 77). Washington, DC: National Academies Press.

Lee, P. J. (2011). Historical literacy and transformative history. In L. Perikleous & D. Shemilt (Eds.), *The future of the past: Why history education matters* (pp. 129 167). Nicosia: The Association for Historical Dialogue and Research/UNDP-ACT.

Legg, R. (2012). Bach, Beethoven, Bourdieu: 'cultural capital' and the scholastic canon in England's A-level examinations. *The Curriculum Journal, 23*(2), 157 172.

Lévesque, S. (2008). *Thinking historically: Educating students for the twenty-first century.* Toronto: University of Toronto Press.

Levstick, L. (2011). Learning history. In R. E. Mayer & P. A. Alexander (Eds.), *The handbook of research on learning and instruction* (pp. 108 126). London: Routledge.

Mandler, P. (2013). History, national life and the new curriculum. Retrieved from http://www.schoolshistoryproject.org.uk/ResourceBase/downloads/MandlerKeynote2013.pdf

Mitra, S. (2013, June 15). Advent of Google means we must rethink our approach to education: We have a romantic attachment to skills from the past which are no longer relevant on a curriculum for today's children. *The Observer.* Retrieved from http://www.theguardian.com/education/2013/jun/15/schools-teaching-curriculum-education-google

Organisation for Economic Co-operation and Development (OECD). (1995). *Recognition of non-formal and informal learning.* Retrieved from http://www.oecd.org/document/25/0,3746,en 2649 39263238 37136921 1 1 1 1,00.html

Phillips, R. (1998). *History teaching, nationhood and the state: A study in educational politics.* London: Cassell.

Philpott, Ch., & Wright, R. (2012). Teaching, learning and curriculum content. In G. E. McPherson & G. F. Welch (Eds.), *The Oxford handbook of music education, Volume 1* (pp. 441 459). New York: Oxford University Press.

Qualifications and Curriculum Authority. (2007). *History programme of study for key stage 3 and attainment target.* London: Author. Retrieved from http://www.education.gov.uk/schools/teachingandlearning/curriculum/secondary/b00199545/history

Rogers, P. J. (1979). *The new history: Theory into practice.* London: The Historical Association.

Royal Society for the Arts. (n.d.). *Opening minds?* [Online]. Retrieved from http://www.rsaopeningminds.org.uk/<Royal Society for the Arts (RSA)n.d.

Royal Society for the Arts. (2005). *How special are subjects? Are they the best way to structure a curriculum or can we do better?* London: Author.

Sexton, F. (2012). Practitioner challenges working with informal learning pedagogies. *British Journal of Music Education, 29*(1), 7 11.

Shemilt, D. (1980). *History 13-16 evaluation study.* Edinburgh: Holmes McDougall.

Shemilt, D. (1983). The devil's locomotive. *History and Theory, 22*(4), 1 18.

Shuter, P., & Child, J. (1987). *Skills in history, Book 1, Changes.* London: Heinemann Education.

Söderman, J., & Folkestad, G. (2004). How hip-hop musicians learn: Strategies in informal creative music making. *Music Education Research, 6*(3), 313 326.

Van Drie, J., & Van Boxtell, C. (2008). Historical reasoning: Towards a framework for analyzing students' reasoning about the past. *Educational Psychology Review, 20*(2), 87 110.

Williams, W. C. (1995). *Patterson* (revised ed.). New York, NY: New Directions.

Wineburg, S. (2001). *Historical thinking and other unnatural acts: Charting the future of teaching the past.* Philadelphia: Temple University Press.

Wineburg, S. (2007). Unnatural and essential: The nature of historical thinking. *Teaching History, 129,* 6 11.

Wright, R. (2008, July). *Thinking globally, acting locally: Informal learning and social justice in music education.* Paper presented at International Society of Music Education, World Conference, Bologna, Italy.

Curriculum and assessment reform gone wrong: the perfect storm of GCSE English

Tina Isaacs

Department of Curriculum, Pedagogy and Assessment, Institute of Education, University of London, London, UK

> Curriculum and its associated assessment are at the heart of educational systems worldwide. In light of perceived national educational stagnation or decline, as well as of performance in international league tables such as Programme for International Student Assessment (PISA), countries have embarked on curriculum and assessment reforms. This is particularly true in England, where currently wholesale changes are being introduced throughout the system. The curriculum and qualification system in England privileges that which is tested over any other expression of knowledge, which leads teachers to concentrate on teaching what is assessed, either externally through examination papers or internally through coursework. In the summer of 2012, following curriculum and assessment reforms to General Certificate of Secondary Education (GCSE) qualifications, serious concerns were raised about the marking and awarding processes for GCSE English, culminating in legal action. Using that experience as an example of assessment policy and practice gone awry, this article explores the ramifications of rapid qualifications changes and posits that some of the problems that plagued GCSE English in 2012 could be repeated, albeit in different guises, after revised qualifications are introduced in 2015.

Context

The relationship between curriculum and its assessment both internationally and nationally in countries such as the United Kingdom has been much discussed, especially in light of perceived national educational stagnation or decline, as well as of performance in international assessments such as Programme for International Student Assessment (PISA), Trends in International Mathematics and Science Study (TIMSS) and Progress in International Reading Literacy Study (PIRLS). Countries have embarked on major curriculum and assessment reforms in order to rectify these shortcomings; this is particularly true in England, where currently wholesale changes are being introduced throughout the system (Kamens & McNeely, 2010).

Not surprisingly, the consensus among researchers is that assessment, especially high-stakes assessment, drives instruction and defines which elements of the curriculum are emphasised (see, for example, Berry & Adamson, 2011; Daugherty, Black, Ecclestone, James, & Newton, 2011; Harlen, 2009; Hayward & Hutchinson, 2013; Koretz, 2008; Stobart, 2008; Wiliam, 2010; Wyse et al., 2012). The qualifications system in England exacerbates this tendency to privilege that which is tested over any other expression of knowledge (Isaacs, 2010; Isaacs, Zara, & Herbert, 2013), leading teachers to concentrate on teaching that which they surmise will be assessed, either externally through examination papers or internally through coursework (also known as controlled assessment). The following explores the ramifications of assessment policy and practice gone wrong, using the case of the GCSE in English. It employs the metaphor of a perfect storm, which although overused in the popular press, describes well what took place in the summer of 2012 and posits that another storm is in the making for the introduction of new GCSEs in English in 2015.

The meteorological definition of a perfect storm is an exceptionally violent storm arising from a rare combination of adverse factors. The term dates back to the twentieth century and is also commonly used to describe a particularly bad or critical state of affairs arising from a number of negative and unpredictable factors. What took place in the summer of 2012 with the English GCSE was tantamount to a perfect storm – a confluence of factors, most of which had unanticipated negative consequences, that all played together to cause the media and legal storm in the centre of which the qualifications regulator in England, the Office of Qualifications and Examinations Regulation (Ofqual) and the developers of GCSE syllabuses and assessments, known as awarding bodies, found themselves in August and September. While that storm has almost entirely run its course, there are other, not entirely dissimilar storms brewing. What will the examination storm of the future, with the introduction of new accountability measures and new GCSE syllabuses hold for England? The following discussion tries to capture the main – but doubtless not all – factors that contributed to 2012's debacle from a curriculum and assessment development and implementation perspective and then attempts to anticipate the factors that could contribute to future examinations upheaval. Curriculum and assessment policy features as well, since assessment development does not take place within a political vacuum. While the narrative is situated in England, education reform through curriculum and assessment changes have a large impact on practitioners everywhere, and while some systems, such as Ontario and Finland, carry out their reforms in a measured and thought-through manner, others, such as some US states in reaction to No Child Left Behind legislation and more currently the advent of Common Core State Standards, introduce changes more hastily.

Because of its topical nature – changes were still being made to GCSE qualifications at the time of this writing in December 2013 – the arguments presented in this article rely heavily on analyses of public speeches, policy papers, DfE and Ofqual consultations and their results, media accounts and my own personal experiences as an employee of Qualifications and Curriculum Authority (QCA) and Ofqual between 1997 and 2009. Where evidence comes from the last, I have tried to make clear in the text that this is my personal knowledge.

The perfect storm: English GCSE 2012

GCSEs are qualifications that students in England take at the end of lower secondary schooling, usually at age 16. They are graded from A* to G, although only grades A* to C are considered a good pass (Isaacs, 2010). A typical student will take eight or nine GCSEs, generally including English, mathematics and science; each of these subjects has a national curriculum programme of study that defines it. School accountability measures revolve around what percentage of students achieves grades C and above in English and mathematics, so the GCSEs in those subjects are particularly high stakes. Assessment of GCSEs is both external (set and marked by the awarding bodies) and internal (set and/or marked by teachers); the proportion is dependent on the subject, with GCSE English during the period this essay concentrates upon having a high proportion of internal assessment, i.e. 60%. After many years of a steadily increasing proportion of students achieving the all important grades C and above in English GCSE, in the summer of 2012 the overall proportion decreased.

When the 2012 results were announced it transpired that 1.5% fewer students in England, Wales and Northern Ireland got grade C and above in GCSE English and English language combined. While that seems a small change, in a cohort of almost 600,000 students that means over 7500 fewer students did not achieve a gatekeeper grade that can help them progress to further and higher education and to some forms of employment. Exacerbating the problem was the fact that the difference in results was not uniform – some schools saw significant increases, others significant decreases in their students' outcomes (Ofqual, 2012) with sometimes potentially serious consequences for the latter because the English government judges a school's success by how many of its students gain five or more GCSEs grades C and above including English and mathematics. Many schools had predicted much higher results for their students and were furious about the outcomes, accusing both the awarding bodies and especially Ofqual of fixing the results. Local authorities, schools, teachers and students banded together and sought a judicial review, claiming that two of the awarding bodies had been unfair in their awarding (Royal Courts of Justice, 2013). Ofqual was named as a secondary party. In the end, the judge found against the claimants, but not before much damage had been done to the credibility of the qualifications in the eyes of the public.[1] The reasons for the 2012 outcomes are complex and somewhat technical. However, the following will try to capture some of the major contributing factors, not solely to explain the past, but to warn about the future.[2]

In September 2010, one year after almost all other subjects, new GCSEs in English were taught for the first time, with first full examination in 2012. These new qualifications contained a range of elements that contributed to the perfect storm. This article attempts to explain some of those that mattered most:

- changes to the number of syllabuses;
- fraying of three-country regulation;
- the inclusion of functional English;
- a new programme of study;
- changes to the structure of the qualifications;
- shifting patterns of entry;
- changes to the qualification's structure;
- changes to the weighting of controlled assessment (coursework);
- the challenge of setting standards in new qualifications;
- teacher behaviour;
- using a comparable outcomes framework to inhibit grade inflation.

Table 1 presents a brief overview of the curriculum and assessment changes made to the English GCSEs, highlighting those that contributed to the perfect storm.

Three syllabuses where there had been two

Before 2008 almost all students in England took GCSE English, which covered the entire programme of study – the mandatory curriculum – for English; just over 75% of students also took English literature (Joint Council for Qualifications [JCQ], 2012). On the whole it was the less able students who did not take English literature and it was they who took the less demanding Foundation tier English, which restricts grades to C through G.

Hoping to introduce more communications and other 'relevant' skills without undermining the traditional aspects of English, some of the developers of the new GCSEs wanted to split the programme of study between a new qualification – English language – and English literature. However,

Table 1. Changes to GCSE English and English literature 2010.

Issue	Prior to 2010	2010 changes
Number of syllabuses	Two syllabuses: English and English literature. The latter covered the entire English Programme of Study for key stage 4.	Three syllabuses: English, English language and English literature. The first covered the entire English Programme of Study for key stage 4 in England. The last two between them covered the programme of study.
Functional English	Functional Skills English did not exist before 2010, therefore there was no explicit weighting attached to elements of functional English.	Required weighting of 45%–55% English and English language attributed to elements of functional English.
New programme of study	Eight-page programme of study outlining in detail what should be taught in speaking, listening, group discussion, drama, reading and writing. Includes a full list of authors.	Streamlined programme of study with less prescription for teachers but also less common material. New emphasis on English language skills within real-life contexts. Spelling, grammar and presentation skills highlighted.
Structure	Linear structure, with assessment at the end of the 2-year course. Resits include all examination papers.	Modular structure with four units the assessment of which can be taken in January and June of both the first and second years. Each module can be resat once. 40% of the assessment must be at the end of the second year.
Controlled assessment (coursework)	Coursework = 40%:20% speaking and listening; 20% writing	Controlled assessment = 60%:20% speaking and listening; 40% writing.

because of different national curriculum requirements across the three countries that shared GCSE provision – England, Wales and Northern Ireland – a compromise was agreed. A new English language GCSE would be created, but another qualification called English would also be developed. The former would not cover the entire programme of study and would emphasise communications and language aspects; the latter would, like its predecessor qualification, cover the entire programme of study. In England, in order to cover the entire programme of study students could choose between a combination of English language and English literature or just take English. In the summer of 2012 about 70% of students in England took the two-qualification combination (JCQ, 2012).

The dilemma facing teachers was which students to put in for the two-qualification programme and which to put in for the single English GCSE. That decision was made even more complicated by the fact that English has tiered (higher and foundation level) examination papers, therefore a second choice had to be made both for English language and English about which tier to enter students for. While neither the JCQ, nor the individual awarding bodies report out results by tier of entry, Assessment and Qualifications Alliance (AQA), which has the most candidates for the English suite (over 60% of the cohort) reported that of the 96,296 candidates in English GCSE only 31.3% gained a grade C or above, while of the 285,620 English language candidates 74.7% gained a grade C or above. For English literature, AQA had 276,198 candidates of whom 76.6% got grade C or above (AQA, 2013). Clearly, less able students only took English. The implications of the switch from two syllabuses to three, most importantly which part of the cohort would be entered for which one(s), could not be fully predicted although it was expected that the sort of students who had not taken English literature in the past would be the most likely students to take only English in 2012.

Three-country regulation

Until May 2013, when Secretary of State for Education in England, Michael Gove, and his counterparts in Wales and Northern Ireland, Leighton Andrews and John O'Dowd, respectively, seemed to abandon it, it was a political 'given' that every possible effort would be made to maintain regulation of GCSEs (and A levels, the qualifications taken by 17 and 18 year olds) across the three countries. In 2006 and 2007, this meant careful negotiations around requirements for English literature – would Shakespeare be required? Could Wales demand the inclusion of Welsh literature and poetry? – as well as around the status of English language GCSE. Both Wales and Northern Ireland were comfortable with offering only two syllabuses – language and literature – and that is what they ended up doing, but in England there was deep concern about the minority of students who might not take the combination of both syllabuses. The concern centred on whether or not these students would be taught the entire key stage 4 programme of study if the only qualification they took was English Language GCSE (which seemed the more likely of the two to be taken). The compromise was the development of three syllabuses (see above), one of which, English, would cover the entire programme of study. Candidates in Wales and Northern Ireland were, however, only allowed to do English language and English literature GCSEs. GCSE English was on offer to schools in England through the three English awarding bodies, AQA, Edexcel and Oxford, Cambridge and RSA Examinations (OCR) and by the Welsh awarding body, Welsh Joint Education Committee (WJEC).

The inclusion of functional English

Very little has been written about the impact of including functional English (and functional mathematics) in the GCSE syllabuses. During the time that the new GCSEs were being developed in 2006 and 2007, the QCA and the Government were promoting and piloting new qualifications called Functional Skills English and Functional Skills Mathematics. At one point the Government was demanding that no one get a grade C or above in GCSE English and mathematics who had not separately passed these new qualifications. Ofqual in 2007 strongly recommended against having the outcomes of one qualification dependent on the outcomes of another, so the compromise agreed to was that English and English language GCSE would contain a 45% to 55% weighting for the functional elements of English (Ofqual, 2011b, 2011c). It can certainly be argued that the functional skills criteria, which include speaking, listening and communication; reading; and writing completely complement the English criteria, but they do have a slightly different slant, emphasising functionality and application in 'purposeful contexts and scenarios that reflect real-life situations' (Ofqual, 2011a, p. 15). What effect changes to English assessment the inclusion of functional elements might be could not be predicted, for example, how much would the assessments need to change and would teachers need to prepare their students for assessments in a different way from before?

A new programme of study

Aside from the addition of functional English, both English and English language syllabuses contained new material, stemming from changes to the English programme of study. While overall the statutory requirements for key stage 4 English were streamlined, reducing prescription for teachers, there was far less potential for crossover work between English language and English literature GCSEs than there had been for English and English literature GCSEs.

When content changes, teachers have to modify their lessons and create new ones. In addition, despite having sample assessment material for the new qualification, they cannot be as certain as when teaching on an older qualification how all of the content will be assessed. And while in the past the same novels, poetry, etc. could be used for both English and English literature GCSE assignments, the new arrangements forbade that, although some of the assessment for English and English language GCSE overlapped (see below). One of the teaching and learning challenges that remained unchanged from the older programme of study was finding the time to cover it in its entirety in the single English GCSE.

Modular assessment

In a paper on revisions to the GCSE criteria addressed to the QCA executive committee in June 2007, this author and head of the Qualification Division Mary Curnock Cook wrote that 'in general terms, we are keen to promote unitisation of GCSEs' (unpublished QCA executive meeting decision paper, 4 June 2007, p. 3). Although I had serious reservations, mainly because I believed that students would be overburdened by assessment, there was enormous pressure at the time to align as many qualifications as possible with the new diploma qualifications, which were completely unitised (see Isaacs, 2013). The executive committee paper did warn that with unitised qualifications assessment could become fragmented and that students might resit modules in order to gain a grade C, 'especially for schools wanting to push their league table positions to the maximum' (p. 4). The solution proffered was to put in place a one resit rule and to have a substantial part of the assessment at the end of the course. What was not anticipated was that the very act of modularisation (resits notwithstanding) means that students will take some of the assessments during the first year and a half of the course and the outcomes of those assessments will be 'banked' toward the final aggregated total. Many schools chose to have students take their external examinations at least once before the end of the course (see below). A compounding factor was that the awarding bodies developed the unitised qualifications in such a way as to allow the controlled assessment (coursework) units for English and English language GCSE to be identical, leading teachers to believe that the cut scores, or grade boundaries, would be identical for both.

Shifting entry patterns

In June 2010, ministers allowed all state schools to offer International GCSE (IGCSE), which up until then had mainly been the preserve of independent schools. One of the main attractions of the IGCSE was that coursework was optional; the qualifications, which are assessed in a linear fashion, also had a reputation for being more demanding than GCSEs. For the 2011–2012 academic year Ofqual reported that about 23,000 fewer students from independent and selective schools took GCSEs than the year before. Many of these students would have achieved the highest (A* and A) grades and taking them out of the overall GCSE cohort would have pulled down overall achievement. In the summer of 2011 16.8% of candidates got an A or A* grade; in 2012 the figure was 15.0% (JCQ, 2012).

Increased weighting for controlled assessment (coursework)

GCSE criteria were revised in 2007. The underlying principle was that controlled assessment would be included only where aspects of the curriculum could not be assessed by external examinations. The author at the time of the revisions was head of the 14-19 qualifications team at QCA and was therefore intimately involved in the work. Initially, working with subject associations and awarding bodies, the 14-19 qualifications team recommended to the QCA executive that the amount of controlled assessment should vary from subject to subject according to what proportion of content was deemed necessary to assess via internal assessment. In the spring of 2007, shortly before the official consultation on GCSE criteria, the executive rejected that recommendation because it was too complex and decided that there would only be three possible weightings for controlled assessment: 0%, 25% and 60%. Respondents to the consultation disagreed with the executive by a small majority (47% versus 44%), wishing to remain more flexible, but the decision remained unchanged (QCA, 2007). For subjects such as English and English language, this weighting decision would prove problematic. Whereas coursework had counted for 40% (20% speaking and listening and 20% writing) now it either had to be 25%, which subject specialists believed was too little, or 60%, which might overbalance the internally assessed aspects. The latter was deemed more in keeping with the subject demands, with speaking and listening remaining at 20% of the overall grade. Historically, as well as in 2012, candidates have received high marks for the speaking and listening component; the evidence produced is largely ephemeral, which makes it difficult for awarding bodies to moderate and possibly adjust if necessary.

Setting standards rather than maintaining them

Compounding all of the factors above, the awarding bodies and Ofqual were faced with the difficult task of setting overall qualification standards for the first time in January 2012. Setting standards is a much more challenging exercise than maintaining them, because of the newness of the qualification and the effects that can have on teacher preparation and implementation and on student response. 'Standard setting is perhaps the branch of psychometrics that blends more artistic, political, and cultural ingredients into the mix of its products than any other' (AERA/APA/NCME Standards 1999, quoted in Cizek & Bunch, 2006, p. 19). While using a blend of examiner judgement and statistics – as is done in the maintenance of standards – when initially setting standards, awarders have to make decisions on student performances that may be different from past performances, because, as with GCSE English, structure and content may be different and weightings of constituent parts may have changed. The challenge in this case was exacerbated by the fact that the initial standard setting was made on very few pre-summer 2012 entries.

Teacher behaviour

It was teacher behaviour, however, that got most of the attention in the summer and autumn of 2012. Before trying briefly to explain that behaviour, it is critical to remind ourselves that GCSE English – like GCSE Mathematics – is not only a gateway subject for students, who cannot enrol on certain post-16 courses without a grade C, get into certain universities or enter certain professions such as teaching, but it is the main accountability measure for schools and the teachers within those schools. Consciously or subconsciously, teachers want as many students as possible to obtain that iconic grade and unlike GCSE Mathematics, English is an open-ended, essay-based subject where the best marking criteria in the world cannot (and should not) exactly describe the entirety of student performance. You can always find – and justify – an extra mark or two, and since people's futures depend on it, you are more likely than not to find those marks.

Because of the modular nature of the new qualifications teachers knew far more about what they believed to be the likely outcomes of their students than in the past. Most students took the externally assessed examination paper and speaking and listening assessments before the summer of 2012, so their marks up until then would have been known prior to the date by which teachers had to submit their marks for the controlled writing assessment. The other 'known' element was the outcomes of the January 2012 standard setting, for which the cut scores (boundary marks between grades) for the controlled writing assessment awarded in January were published. English coursework cut scores for grades in the past had been remarkably stable and there was no obvious reason why teachers would believe that things would be different this time around. But there is no guarantee that a certain number of marks will push a student over a grade boundary – cut scores can, do and did change between January and June awarding.

According to the Ofqual report (Ofqual, 2012), teachers, knowing the outcomes of their students' examinations because the students had taken those examinations in earlier sessions, and assuming that the cut scores for the controlled assessment from January would be relatively stable, found those extra marks that would give their students a C (or B, A or A*) grade overall. The most telling evidence that Ofqual brought to bear was two charts showing the how the outcomes for AQA English language would have been different had the cut scores required to achieve a grade C not changed between January and June 2012. In the chart that showed what grades might have been in the June assessments had the boundaries remained unchanged from January, the peaks of student performance at grades C, B and A sat comfortably within the grade boundaries, but in the chart that reflected the actual outcomes, the peaks shift over to the left and many students whose overall marks would have got them a grade C in January, got a grade D in June. As mentioned previously, while overall the percentage of students achieving a grade C or better was only 1.5% lower in 2012 than 2011, the pattern was dramatically different in different schools.

Using comparable outcomes to set standards

QCA and now Ofqual have adopted a comparable outcomes approach to set, and in the early years of a qualification, maintain, standards. Comparable outcomes basically means that all things being equal, based on information on prior performance, the proportion of students who obtained certain grades this year should be the same as the proportion who achieved them last year. Setting comparable outcomes is largely a statistical, normative exercise. This is in contrast with comparable performance, where how well students achieved each year is the point of comparison and relies to a greater extent on examiner judgement than comparable outcomes.

With comparable performance, you would expect students in the first year of a qualification to do worse than students the year before, who benefitted from known syllabuses and teachers comfortable teaching on them. But after that initial decrease, the proportion of students getting good grades could increase steadily as everyone becomes used to the new syllabuses. That, plus the very human tendency of awarders to give students the benefit of the doubt when setting cut scores, leads inexorably to grade inflation.

A comparable outcomes approach rectifies this situation, because it keeps the proportion of grades stable. There can be variation, of course, but that variation can be both up and down. Awarding bodies have to make a case to Ofqual if the outcomes of a qualification are significantly different from those predicted.

In the case of GCSE English 2012 the final outcomes were pretty much in line with the expected comparable outcomes predictions. However, the grade boundaries, especially for written controlled assessments were notably different. Had the grade boundaries for the June assessment been the same as for the January ones, there would have been a 20% increase in the proportion of students gaining a grade C and above (Ofqual, 2012), which might have strained the credibility of the qualification, especially given that students tend to do worse, rather than better in the first year of a qualification.

The gathering storm: GCSE English from 2015

Many of these factors could cause trouble again when the new GCSEs in English, English literature and mathematics come on board starting in 2015, although some factors, such as modular assessment, will no longer exist, and about others lessons seem to have been learned. However, I believe that other unanticipated factors may arise and will try to elaborate on some of them using GCSE English as the starting point, although some of the difficulties could happen in other subjects. Any adjustments that the awarding bodies and/or Ofqual make in light of issues arising will, however, be slightly easier to keep out of the limelight because the linear nature of the new assessment regime.

The number of syllabuses

It appears as though the lesson about the proliferation of different syllabuses has been learned. The Government's response to Ofqual's GCSE consultation stated that there would be separate language and literature qualifications, but no combined option (Department for Education (DfE), 2013c). What is not clear is whether this means that all students will have to take both GCSEs in order to cover the revised programme of study. At the time of this writing the draft programme of study for key stage 4 English was out for consultation until February 2014; therefore it is impossible to tell with any level of certainty whether a student will be taught the entire programme of study if s/he is enrolled on English language GCSE alone. However, that draft programme of study makes clear that students should read whole texts in specific areas (at least one play by Shakespeare; works from the nineteenth, twentieth, and twenty-first centuries and poetry since 1789, including representative romantic poetry). Separately, subject criteria for English language and English literature GCSEs were consulted upon in the summer of 2013, with specified literature requirements (at least one play by Shakespeare, at least one nineteenth-century novel, a selection of poetry since 1789, including representative romantic poetry and fiction or drama from the British Isles from 1914 onwards) only contained within the latter (DfE, 2013b). Entry patterns across the cohort cannot be predicted at this point. Because the standard of demand will be higher (see below) on all GCSEs, schools may be less likely to put lower-achieving students in for English literature GCSE, instead concentrating on English language GCSE, which will count towards overall accountability measures. However, if regulations allow for crossover reading, as in the pre-2010 syllabuses, entry for English literature may remain high.

Three-country regulation

As of May 2013, three-country regulation is dead. Michael Gove wrote to his counterparts that 'the time is right for us to acknowledge the three-country regulation of GCSEs and A-levels is no longer an objective towards which we should be working' (Coughlan, 2013). Wales and Northern Ireland have decided not to accept content, structural and grading changes to GCSEs (and A levels) (see below), which could lead to very different qualifications being called by the same title across the three countries. This will make comparability judgements across the qualifications very difficult, which will cause new problems for end users such as employers and university admissions tutors. Unlike Scotland, which has an entirely different system, Wales, Northern Ireland and England all want to keep the GCSE brand – the outstanding and at the moment irresolvable question is whether that is possible for qualifications with deliberately different standards.

Functional English

The new draft English programme of study on the DfE website is almost silent about elements stressed in functional English qualifications. For example, the words 'daily world' and 'real life' are absent, although they featured prominently in the 2007 English programme of study. Instead there is a renewed emphasis on spelling, punctuation, grammar and using standard English. Functional English elements are also absent from the subject criteria for English language GCSE first published in June 2013. Spoken language, which featured prominently in functional English, will be unweighted, although assessed, in the new GCSEs (see below; this new assessment arrangement will begin in the summer of 2014 on the current syllabuses). It appears that the link between functional skills and GCSEs has been almost entirely broken; however, there is a new requirement in England that if a student does not obtain a good pass in GCSE English (or mathematics) s/he will have to continue studying the subject post-16. The assumption is that students will continue taking GCSEs, but substituting functional skills qualifications has yet to be ruled out.

(*Another*) *new programme of study*

A draft programme of study for English appeared on the DfE website in February 2013; it was subsequently revised and went out for consultation in December 2013, but it is not clear when it will be finalised. Returning to a measure of prescription, the draft programme of study, as highlighted above, contains a list of literature that students must read in key stage 4: at least one play by Shakespeare; works from the nineteenth, twentieth and twenty-first centuries and poetry since 1789, including representative romantic poetry (DfE, 2013a). This is both an increase in the amount of literature students must read and a shift from contemporary literature to the English-language classics. Allusions to authors' craft, cultural diversity, multimodal study and connections to the real world and daily life have disappeared; added in is a specific section on grammar and vocabulary. Speaking and listening has changed to spoken English. Once again, teachers will need to modify what they teach and how they teach it. And awarding bodies will need quite quickly to incorporate any changes into the specifications that will need to have gone through the full accreditation process by September 2014.

Shifting entry patterns

It is impossible to predict whether or not the high-performing students in the independent sector will return once new GCSEs are in place in 2015. In the summer of 2013 there was a dramatic increase in the number of students sitting IGCSEs (numbers increased in English language from 18,000 in the summer of 2012 to 78,000 in the summer of 2013) (Ofqual, 2013c). When the course is more demanding (see below), linear, 100% externally assessed and does not incorporate speaking and listening in the outcomes some independent and selective schools may return to the fold. However, it is also possible that other schools will abandon the qualifications entirely – free schools and academies do not have to follow the national curriculum and no one has to do GCSE qualifications (although most do). It is entirely possible that the cohort may once again shift and the direction of that shift is not predictable at a time when even moderate organisations such as the National Association of Head Teachers have passed no confidence votes in Mr. Gove's education policies.

Weighting of controlled assessment

In its response to Ofqual's consultation on GCSEs, the Government stated that it wanted the qualifications' 'internal assessment kept to a minimum and used only where there is a compelling case to do so' (DfE, 2013c, p. 8). Communication in English was one of the areas where respondents had identified that internal assessment would be necessary and Government seems to have accepted that. However, Ofqual has announced that speaking and listening will no longer be aggregated into the overall English grade but will instead be reported out separately (Ofqual, 2013a), the impact of which is unpredictable but is likely to lower students' overall achievement since most do very well on this element (Ofqual, 2012). Given how much controlled assessment (coursework) contributed to the debacle of 2012 it is unsurprising that Ofqual has decided that both English language and English literature GCSEs will contain 100% external assessment (Ofqual, 2013b). While that, coupled with linear assessment, resolves many of the summer of 2012's problem, if there is no coursework or assessed extended writing, an argument could be made that the construct of English is not being adequately assessed, even if the subject criteria demand that students learn to write effectively for different audiences, take notes, write drafts, revise, edit and proofread (DfE, 2013b). The confines of a timed assessment pretty much preclude all of these essential subject elements and most schools will concentrate on the areas of the curriculum that are assessed.

Standard setting/comparable outcomes

Mr. Gove has clearly stated that the new GCSEs will be more demanding than those now in place especially at the equivalents of grades C and A/A*. He left it to Ofqual to decide how to do so, indicated that a different grading structure may be needed. Ofqual (2013b) has developed a new grading system, using numbers rather than letter grades to denote achievement. In the future, GCSEs will be graded from 9 to 1, with 9 denoting the highest achievement. It will not be possible to equate the new numbering system with the old letter grading system because there is one extra grading point; it will, however, be possible to introduce a grade 10 in the future should too many students achieve 9s. Mr. Gove also wanted Ofqual to minimise the number of GCSEs that are tiered and originally also wanted, for English language (and mathematics) GCSEs, awarding bodies to report out on achievement across the different elements, i.e. reading, writing and speaking, so that those who need to continue to retake GCSEs post-16 will know where to put the most effort (DfE, 2013c). Ofqual has concluded that only Mathematics and Science GCSEs will be tiered, but has not mandated reporting out achievement across elements; this would be extremely difficult in a compensatory qualification where good performance in part of an assessment can compensate for less good performance in other parts (Ofqual, 2013b).

Introducing new GCSEs with so many differences from what went before raises the setting standards issue once again, only this time it will be much more difficult. Comparable outcomes, strictly speaking, must be off the table, since the Government has expressly demanded that outcomes not be comparable, and one would expect that by raising standards fewer students will achieve the highest grades.

How are standards to be set, especially in a qualification such as English that is graded by the quality of outcomes rather than by more demanding content? Although new, required reading can be more demanding, is *Hard Times* or *A Christmas Carol* (both nineteenth-century novels) more demanding than *Ulysses*? Standards are more likely to reside in a combination of changes to mark schemes and an adjustment of marker judgement; reliability – especially inter-rater reliability – will be a thorny issue here. With untiered assessments both the reading lists and the wording of the questions set could be affected – will they both need to be accessible to what are now foundation-level students or will those students' needs be ignored because of the need to increase demand?

Finally, what about the time line? Ofqual recently announced that only Mathematics and English GCSEs will be ready for first teaching in September 2015, which takes some of the pressure off other subjects. However, before September 2014 a new national curriculum has to be ratified, with any necessary post-consultation changes made, awarding bodies have to develop syllabuses, Ofqual has to accredit them. This is quite a large amount of work that needs to take place in a short period of time. Piloting will obviously be impossible, so if any issues arise they will need to be dealt with during the first years of the course.

Just like in 2012.

Notes

1. The Welsh Assembly ordered the awarding body for Wales, WJEC, to regrade all of its candidates who lived in Wales, which meant that with the same raw marks a student living in Cardiff might have got a C, while one living in Carlisle could have got a D.
2. Because I worked for QCA and then Ofqual as head of the 14 19 Team and head of the 14 19 regulation, respectively, some of the following account is from first hand experience rather than published papers.

References

AQA. (2013). *Results statistics*. Retrieved from http://web.aqa.org.uk/exams-office/about-results/results-statistics.php

Berry, R., & Adamson, B. (2011). Assessment reform past, present and future. In R. Berry & B. Adamson (Eds.), *Assessment reform in education in the Asia-Pacific region: Issues, concerns and prospects* (Vol. 14, pp. 3 14). London: Springer.

Cizek, G. J., & Bunch, M. (2006). *A guide to establishing and evaluating performance standards on tests*. Thousand Oaks, CA: Sage.

Coughlan, S. (2013, May 21). UK shared exam system faces break up. *BBC News*. Retrieved from http://www.bbc.co.uk/news/education-22609674

Daugherty, R., Black, P., Ecclestone, K., James, M., & Newton, P. (2011). Assessment of significant learning outcomes. In R. Berry & B. Adamson (Eds.), *Assessment reform in education in the Asia-Pacific region: Issues, concerns and prospects* (Vol. 14, pp. 165 183). London: Springer.

Department for Education. (2013a). *English programme of study for key stage 4*. Retrieved from https://www.gov.uk/government/uploads/system/uploads/attachment data/file/262167/English KS4 PoS Draft.pdf.

Department for Education. (2013b). *Reformed GCSE subject content consultation*. Retrieved from https://www.gov.uk/government/uploads/system/uploads/attachment data/file/254513/GCSE consultation-government s response.pdf

Department for Education. (2013c). *Reforming key stage 4 qualifications consultation government response*. Retrieved from http://media.education.gov.uk/assets/files/pdf/r/reforming%20key%20stage%204%20qualifications%20consultation%20response%20final%20-%20with%20new%20annex%20b.pdf

Harlen, W. (2009). Improving assessment of learning and for learning. *Education, 37*, 247 257.

Hayward, E. L., & Hutchinson, C. (2013). 'Exactly what do you mean by consistency?' Exploring concepts of consistency and standards in Curriculum for Excellence in Scotland. *Assessment in Education: Principles, Policy & Practice, 20*, 53 68.

Isaacs, T. (2010). Educational assessment in England. *Assessment in Education: Principles, Policy & Practice, 17*, 315 334.

Isaacs, T. (2013). The diploma qualification in England: An avoidable failure? *Journal of Vocational Education and Training, 65*, 277 290.

Isaacs, T., Zara, C., & Herbert, G. (2013). *Key concepts in educational assessment*. London: Sage.

Joint Council for Qualifications. (2012). *Provisional GCSE results June 2012*. Retrieved from http://www.jcq.org.uk/Download/examination-results/gcses/gcse

Kamens, D. H., & McNeely, C. (2010). Globalization and the growth of international educational testing and national assessment. *Comparative Education Review, 54*(1), 5 25.

Koretz, D. (2008). *Measuring up: What educational testing really tells us*. Cambridge, MA: Harvard University Press.

Office of Qualifications and Examinations Regulation. (2011a). *Functional skills criteria for English entry 1, entry 2, entry 3, level 1 and level 2*. Retrieved from http://ofqual.gov.uk/documents/functional-skills-criteria-for-english/

Office of Qualifications and Examinations Regulation. (2011b). *Subject criteria for English GCSE*. Retrieved from http://ofqual.gov.uk/documents/gcse-subject-criteria-for-english/

Office of Qualifications and Examinations Regulation. (2011c). *Subject criteria for English Language GCSE*. Retrieved from http://ofqual.gov.uk/documents/gcse-subject-criteria-for-english-language/

Office of Qualifications and Examinations Regulation. (2012). *GCSE English 2012*. Retrieved from http://www.ofqual.gov.uk/files/2012-11-02-gcse-english-final-report-and-appendices.pdf

Office of Qualifications and Examinations Regulation. (2013a). *Our announcement on speaking and listening assessments*. Retrieved from http://ofqual.gov.uk/blog/our-announcement-on-speaking-and-listening-assessments

Office of Qualifications and Examinations Regulation. (2013b). *Reforms to GCSEs in England from 2015.* Retrieved from http://ofqual.gov.uk/documents/summary-on-reforms-to-gcses-from-2015

Office of Qualifications and Examinations Regulation. (2013c). *Why GCSEs may look different this year.* Retrieved from http://ofqual.gov.uk/files/2013-08-22-annex-a-summer-2013-why-gcses-may-look-different-this-year.pdf

Qualifications and Curriculum Authority. (2007). *GCSE qualification and subject criteria consultation summary report.* Retrieved from http://webarchive.nationalarchives.gov.uk/20091002201257/http://qcda.gov.uk/libraryAssets/media/qca-07-3473_gcse_criteria_consultation_report.pdf

Royal Courts of Justice. (2013). *LB Lewishassm & Ors v AQA, Edexcel, Ofqual & Ors.* Retrieved from http://www.judiciary.gov.uk/Resources/JCO/Documents/Judgments/london-borough-lewisham-aqa-judgment-13022013.pdf

Stobart, G. (2008). *Testing times: The uses and abuses of assessment.* Abingdon: Routledge.

Wiliam, D. (2010). Standardized testing and school accountability. *Educational Psychologist, 45,* 107–122.

Wyse, D., Baumfield, V., Egan, D., Hayward, L., Hulme, M., Menter, I., Lingard, B. (2012). *Creating the curriculum.* Abingdon: Routledge.

Index

Abbott, T. 101–2
absolutism 8
academies 142
accountability 50, 68, 90–1, 95–6, 100–2, 104–6, 124, 130–1, 138, 141
action research 117–18
adversarial systems 124
aesthetics 39
aims 1–5, 7, 10, 75–88, 121–2, 124
Alexander, R. 11, 110–11, 124
alienation 119, 121
Allsup, R.E. 119–21, 123
American National Research Council 113
Andrews, L. 134
anti-realism 29, 33
Apple, M. 31
Aristotle 77, 114
arithmetic 98
Arnold, M. 3
Asia 1, 103
assessment 63, 65, 69, 92–4, 96–9, 103–4, 112, 129–46
Assessment and Qualifications Alliance (AQA) 134–5
assumptions 7, 33, 35, 42–3, 51, 59, 115, 141
astronomy 82
Australia 10, 89–109, 117
Australian Council for Educational Research (ACER) 95
Australian Curriculum 89–109
Australian Curriculum, Assessment and Reporting Authority (ACARA) 10–11, 100
authenticity 121
autonomous instrumentalism 18
awarding bodies 130–2, 135–7, 139–40, 142–3

Barton, C. 81
Beattie, P. 96
Berliner, D. 69
Bernstein, B. 3, 8, 35, 52, 89–90, 93, 101, 103–4, 122–3
Biesta, G. 8–9, 28–48, 93–4

biology 10, 82, 85–6
bipolar constructions 110–28
Bligh, A. 95–6
Bloor, D. 39
Borbidge, R. 96
Brandom, R. 23
British Educational Research Association 3
Butler, P.H. 80

Cain, T. 11, 110–28
Canada 117
capitalism 120
Cartesian Anxiety 35, 42
catchment areas 7
Catholics 92
Centre on Organization and Restructuring of Schools 96
Chapman, A. 11, 110–28
chemistry 10, 83, 85, 95
China 69
Cigman, R. 7
citizenship 30, 50, 52, 54, 59, 66, 78–81, 90, 93–4, 97–8, 100
class 31, 99, 101, 123
classification 3
co-ordination 8, 29–30, 42–5
coding frameworks 57–8
cognitive knowledge 14–15
Common Core State Standards 131
common sense 44
Conservative-Liberal Democrat government 2
consumerism 80
control 1–5, 36, 38–9, 41, 94–5, 100, 119–20, 122–3
controlled assessment *see* coursework
Cook, M.C. 136
coordination 8, 29–30, 36–7, 42, 45
Copernican turn 35
Counsell, C. 113
coursework 130, 132, 136–8, 142–3
creating curricula 1–5
Creationism 43

INDEX

critical instrumentalism 181
critical realism 13, 23–5
culture 3, 17, 35, 50, 66–7; Australia 92, 97–8, 105; culture wars 31; GCSE English 138, 142; history/music 114, 121, 123; science 80, 82
Cunningham, M. 68
curricular design 62–4, 68, 89–109
curriculum 1–5, 11; aims 75–88; co-ordination 42–5; curriculum studies 1–3, 5, 8, 31; development 75–88; dichotomies 110–28; downgraded 49–74; GCSE English 129–46; and knowledge 13–28; new 49–74; pragmatism 28–48; scope 6–12
Curriculum for Excellence (CfE) 50, 53–69, 93
cut scores 138–9

Darwinism 43
databases 57
Dawkins, J. 100
Definition and Selection of Competencies (DeSeCo) 51
democracy 1, 78–81, 105, 122
Department for Education (DfE) 131, 141–2
Derry, J. 19, 23
Descartes, R. 34
Dewey, J. 2, 8, 29, 31, 33–40, 43–5, 52, 94, 98–9, 114, 119
dichotomies 11, 110–28
differentiation 10
dispositions 9, 14–15, 18, 52, 78–9, 86, 89–90, 93–4, 101, 104–5
document analysis 56–8, 64–7
dualism 34, 39, 43
Duncan, A. 1
Durkheim, E. 6, 9, 29

ecology 79
economic instrumentalism 18
economics 18, 97
Edexcel 135
education 1–5; aims 76–88; Australia 89–109; curriculum scope 6–12; GCSE English 129–46; history/music 110–28; knowledge 13–28; pragmatism 28–48; science 75–88; Scotland/New Zealand 49–74
elites 123
engineering 84
England 2–4, 10, 12, 67–8, 76; and Australia 93; GCSE English 130–1, 134–5, 141; history/music 111–13, 117; science 81–2, 85
English 91, 100, 102, 104, 129–46
epistemology 5, 16–17, 23, 25, 33; epistemic frameworks 8, 13–15, 20–2, 24–5, 115–16; epistemic realism 13, 22, 25; mind-world scheme 34–5; social 20–5

essentialism 17, 21, 24–5
ethics 19, 35, 77, 83, 102
evidence 116, 137
evolution 82–3
examinations 4, 12, 63, 69, 129–46
experience 8, 35–6, 38–42, 54–5, 59, 63, 65–7, 78, 111
experimental learning 36
external factors 7

federalism 91–2, 95, 100
feminism 81
Finland 1, 130
Folkestad, G. 118–20
formalism 114
foundationalism 10, 13, 16–18, 25
Framework Project 97
framing 3, 23, 25, 60, 92, 94, 101, 122–3
free schools 142
Freire, P. 98, 119
fulfilling lives 78
Functional Skills 135, 141
future research 3, 9

GCSEs 4, 12, 129–46
generalisations 16, 78, 119
genericism 50, 113–14, 116
genetics 82
geography 81, 83, 97
geology 83
Gill, S. 52
Gillard, J. 91
Global Education Reform Movement (GERM) 95, 102, 106
globalisation 5, 10, 49, 89–109
Goals for Young Australians 100
Gove, M. 3, 111–12, 134, 141–3
grade inflation 12, 132, 139
Green, L. 117–19, 121–3

habits 3, 15, 36, 39
Hadow Report 111
Hall, S. 98
Hamlyn Foundation 117
Hargreaves, L. 68
Harris, K. 76–7
Hawke, B. 91–2
Hayward, L. 1–5
hedonism 77
hegemony 1, 44
hermeneutics 114–15
Hertfordshire Music Service 117
Higgins, S. 1–5
Hirsch, E.D. 113–15
history 7, 11, 91, 94, 97, 100–4, 110–16, 123–4
History Project 112

INDEX

Howard, J. 94
human capital 92
Hume, D. 34
Hutchins, R.M. 77

ideal types 11
ideology 11–12, 19, 24–5, 101, 112
Index of Community Socio-Educational Advantage (ICSEA) 100
inferentialism 13, 23, 25, 38, 41
informal learning 4, 11, 117–23, 125
Information and Communications Technology (ICT) 121
infrastructure 21
Institute of Education, University of London 2
instrumentalism 13, 18–19, 21, 25, 50, 60–1
intelligent action 36–7
inter-rater reliability 143
interaction 2, 35, 42, 67
interdisciplinarity 51–2
internal factors 7
internalisation 14
International Association for the Evaluation of Educational Achievement (IEA) 95
international comparison 1–3, 9–10, 49–74, 141
International GCSEs (IGCSEs) 136–7, 142
intersubjectivity 42, 45
Isaacs, T. 12, 129–46

Jaffurs, S.E. 118–19
Jakobi, A.P. 51
Jenkins, P. 119–20
Joint Council for Qualifications (JCQ) 134

Keating, P. 91–2
Key Stage 3 117
Key Stage 4 135–6, 140, 142
keyword searches 57
knowledge 1–5; aims 7, 10, 80–1; analysis 49–74; building 8; co-ordination 42–5; and curriculum 10, 13–28; downgrading 9, 50, 53, 56, 58, 67–70, 112; ends/means 59–60; experience 38–40; knowledge economy 96, 102; new curriculum 50–3; politics 31–2; pragmatism 28–48; status 61–3; transactional theory 35–8; transmission 6
Knowledge and Control 3

Lawrence, D.H. 77
leadership 7, 105
Leading Schools 96
league tables 1, 96, 102, 136
learnification 8, 28, 94
lifelong learning 51
Lingard, B. 10, 89–109
literacy 64, 90, 92, 95, 102, 113–14

Livingston, K. 1–5
local authorities 63, 131–2
Locke, J. 77
Longbottom, J.E. 80
Luke, A. 93, 98
Lyotard, F. 94

McGregor, G. 10, 89–109
McIntyre, D. 68
managerialism 68
Masters, G. 95
Masters Report 95
mathematics 1, 7, 31, 55, 60; Australia 91, 95, 100, 102, 104; and GCSE English 131, 135, 138, 140–1, 143; and science 84; Scotland/New Zealand 62, 66–7
media 1, 95–6, 98, 105, 120, 125, 130–1
Melbourne Declaration 93, 100–1, 104–5
metaphysics 21, 24
mind-world scheme 34–5, 41
Minty, S. 63
Mitra, S. 114
modular assessment 50, 136, 138, 140
Moore, R. 9
morality 78
Muller, J. 51
multi-disciplinarity 4
Munn Report 62
music 11, 60, 110, 117–28
Musical Futures 117
My School 96, 100, 102

National Assessment Plan - Literacy and Numeracy (NAPLAN) 90–1, 95–6, 99–106
National Association of Head Teachers 142
natural selection 83
Neill, A.S. 77
neo-traditionalism 111–13, 116
New Basics 10–11, 90–9, 103–6
New History 112–13
new imperialism 1
New Zealand 9, 49–74
New Zealand Curriculum (NZC) 50, 53–63, 65–9
Newman, C. 92
Newmann, F. 96–8
Newton, I. 83, 85
No Child Left Behind 131
normativity 3, 18, 22–3, 26, 82, 118, 120, 139
North America 31
Northern Ireland 131, 134–5, 141
Nozick, R. 34
numeracy 64, 90, 92, 95, 102

Ochs, K. 51
O'Dowd, J. 134

INDEX

OECD 2
Office of Qualifications and Examinations Regulation (Ofqual) 130–2, 135, 137, 139–40, 142–3
Ontario 130
ontology 16, 23–6
Opening Minds 10
Organisation for Economic Cooperation and Development (OECD) 51, 95, 99, 101
outcomes 39, 41, 44, 50, 54; Australia 93, 95–9, 104; GCSE English 131–2, 135–6, 138–40, 142–4; history/music 111, 120, 124; Scotland/New Zealand 56–7, 59–67
Oxford, Cambridge and RSA Examinations (OCR) 135

Peirce, C.S. 19
Pell, T. 68
perfect storm 12, 129–46
performativity 2, 4, 14–15, 50, 95–6, 99–100, 102, 104, 115, 138, 142–3
Peters, R. 76
Phillips, D. 51
philosophy 2–4, 17, 19, 21, 23, 29, 31–4, 41–5, 76, 95, 105, 114
Philpott, C. 122
Physics 10, 69, 83–5, 95
politicisation 31–2, 78–9, 81, 91, 99, 105, 123–4, 138
positivism 8, 17
power structures 3, 20–1, 24, 31, 33, 42, 123
pragmatism 13, 19–22, 25–6, 28–48
Priestley, M. 9–10, 49–74, 93
private sector 95–6
productive learning 11
professionalisation 68, 93, 95, 104
Programme for International Student Assessment (PISA) 1, 15, 99, 105, 129
programmes of study 132, 134–6, 140–2
Progress in International Reading Literacy Study (PIRLS) 129
progressivism 105
psychometrics 138
pupil testing 1, 15, 69, 90–2, 95–6, 99–101, 104
Putnam, H. 22
Pyne, C. 101

qualifications 50, 130–2, 134–8, 140–2
Qualifications and Curriculum Authority (QCA) 136–7, 139
quantum theory 83
Queensland School Reform Longitudinal Study (QSRLS) 92–3, 96–8, 104
Queensland State Education - 2010 96–7
Queensland Studies Authority 104

Rata, E. 51
reading 1, 55, 65–6, 98, 113–16, 135, 143
reflection 37, 53, 112
Reiss, M. 4–7, 10, 75–88
relativism 16, 21, 29, 32–4, 43, 45, 53, 68, 83, 104
relativity 83
rich tasks 93, 97–9
Rousseau, J.-J. 77, 114
Royal Society for the encouragement of Arts, Manufactures and Commerce (RSA) 10
Rudd, K. 91, 94, 99–100

Sahlberg, P. 95
scepticism 34, 41
Schools Council 10, 112
science 1, 8–10, 22, 31, 75–88; Australia 91–2, 95, 100, 102–4; and GCSE English 131, 143; and history/music 114; pragmatism 35, 44–5; Scotland/New Zealand 53, 55, 60–3, 69
science, technology, engineering, mathematics (STEM) subjects 84
Scotland 9, 49–74, 93, 141
Scott, D. 7–9, 13–28
Scottish Executive 53–4
Sellars, W. 14
sex education 85–6
Shakespeare, W. 134, 140, 142
Shieh, E. 121
Sinnema, C. 9–10, 49–74
skills 52, 55, 58, 61–7, 86; Australia 93–4, 97–8, 101–3, 105; GCSE English 135, 141; history/music 111–14, 116, 118, 123–4; skill-based knowledge 10–12, 14–15, 18, 28–9, 31, 91
Smart State 96–7
social constructivism 13, 20, 25, 29, 52–3
social facts 6, 23
social realism 9, 13, 21, 25, 29, 50, 52–3, 60, 67–8
social studies 11, 55, 62, 64, 66–7
socialisation 31
sociology 3–4, 6, 9, 11, 28, 31–2, 44, 85, 89–90, 104
Söderman, J. 119
South African Truth and Reconciliation Commission 33
special interest groups (SIGs) 2
Spencer, H. 31
Standish, P. 76
Studies of Society and the Environment (SOSE) 97
subjectification 31
Swann, M. 68
Sweden 121

INDEX

Teaching and Learning Audits 95–6
technology 33, 42, 44, 59–60, 62–3, 80, 84, 94, 96, 98, 101–2, 105–6
testing *see* pupil testing
thermodynamics 84
Thomson, G. 52
totalitarianism 51
transactional realism 8, 41
transactional theory 8, 22, 30–1, 34–43
Trends in International Maths and Science Study (TIMSS) 95, 129
truth 9, 16–17, 19–20, 33, 38, 40–5, 76

United Kingdom (UK) 31, 129
United States (US) 1, 69, 81, 96, 131
University of Queensland 93
University of Wisconsin-Madison 96

vested interests 21
Vygotsky, L. 22, 98

Wales 76, 81, 131, 134–5, 141
Weber, M. 11
Welsh Joint Education Committee (WJEC) 135
Westerlund, H. 121
Western civilization 35, 68, 77, 84
Wheelahan, L. 52
White, J. 4–7, 10, 15, 75–88
Whitty, G. 52
Williams, M. 17
Williams, W.C. 124
Wineburg, S. 115–16
Wittgenstein, L. 39
Wordsworth, W. 114
Wright, R. 119, 122
writing 55, 65–6, 98, 114, 135, 137
Wyse, D. 1–5

Young, M. 2–3, 6–12, 19, 28–9, 50–1, 53, 67, 94